RIDES OF PASSAGE

Matt and Arthur Lamy

Published by Thirty-Six Books

First published 2016 by Thirty-Six Books

12, Coulsdon Road, Coulsdon, Surrey, CR5 2LA

www.thirty-sixbooks.com

ISBN 978-0-9935874-0-5 HB

All interior image credits: Matt Lamy and Arthur Lamy

Cover design: Callum Tomsett

1 3 5 7 9 8 6 4 2

A CIP catalogue record for this book is available from the
British Library.

Printed in the United Kingdom

www.thirty-sixbooks.com

To Susan and Manda.
Proof that great women can even be found standing
behind a couple of clowns like us.

Contents

RIDES OF PASSAGE

"To get back one's youth, one has merely to repeat one's follies"
Oscar Wilde, *The Picture of Dorian Gray*

Introduction

Many years ago, a truculent teenager (that's me) and a middle-aged man (that's my dad, Arthur) set off on an adventure — not only to cycle across a foreign country where people spoke a different language but also, to make it more challenging, they carried their sleeping quarters and essentials with them.

As a 15-year-old schoolboy living in Jersey I had to complete something called Project Trident. This involved doing three weeks of work experience, volunteering for charity, and undertaking a personal challenge. I could have chosen something a lot less arduous than cycling 600 miles across France, and to begin with the trip was simply going to be a reasonable 250-mile tour around Northern France, almost all within sight of my island home. However, when my three mates who were going to join us fell by the wayside, dad and I decided to attempt something greater. Our French trip grew into a cycle-touring odyssey that crossed the entire country, from Saint Malo on the Channel coast to Sète — a long, long way away — on the shores of the Mediterranean.

The journey had the potential to go very wrong. Dad and I had only ever cycled in Jersey, which has a landmass nine miles by five miles and, as a general rule, when you reach the sea you've gone too far. Even on a bicycle this usually takes less than an hour. But France is a very big place and each day we would cycle further and further from home. To reach the Mediterranean we planned it would take us 10 days, camping and map reading as we went.

In an age before mobiles, we had to use pay phones to call home with updates of our progress and we slept in campsites we found en route. We saw the ever-evolving beauty of a country as it changed from north to south. We met interesting characters and ate good food. We had close shaves with articulated lorries, skidding ambulances and aggressive dogs. But, most importantly, after a week and a half we made it to Sète.

We spent the next two decades boring our loved ones with the occasional 'French story marathon' around the dining table. Then, 21 years later, we had another idea: let's do it again.

Rides of Passage is the result of that idea and, as you will read, our second journey across France was, if anything, a greater challenge than the first.

However, we also wanted this book to be about more than just a father and son cycling across France. Since our original tour, dad and I have had another 21 years' worth of experiences. I have grown from a boy into a man, a husband and a father. Meanwhile the old chap has gone from being a dad to a grandfather and bus-pass holder — although I should point out that at a youthful 63 years old, he is far from pensionable in terms of spirit and temperament. As well as the story of the literal journey as we headed 600 miles south across France, we also wanted to touch on the metaphorical journey of the 21 years that have brought us to our current states.

As it happened, while planning our second trans-France cycle tour I found myself reading *Zen and the Art of Motorcycle Maintenance*. Although hard to entirely sum up, that book is about a father and son's motorcycle road trip across America, interwoven with Buddhist teachings and very 'of its time' 1970s philosophy. The last thing I wanted was to land us knee-deep in pretentious self-indulgence, but I couldn't help thinking: wouldn't it be fun to combine our more realistic — albeit, energetic — road trip with a few easily-relatable life stories and some homespun philosophy. (I even toyed with calling this book *Arf and the Art of Bicycle Maintenance*, but *Rides of Passage* has proved more apt.) While dad and I, separately and together, have undergone a great deal in the last two decades, we don't think our individual experiences are particularly unique. Far from it. If anything, we hope there are many moments in *Rides of Passage* with which every reader can identify.

And that leads me to our other aim with this book. As a journalist, I have interviewed everybody from rock stars and politicians to self-effacing folk without airs or affectations. I can say, without fear of contradiction, that everybody has a story to tell and the tales that have touched me most have always come from people who would, for want of a better term, be called 'normal'.

I firmly believe that every one of us, no matter how humble our lives, has something to say. Yet every day we are pelted with articles and images of what we're told are exceptional people doing what we're told are exceptional things. Celebrity gossip columns and Sunday newspaper magazines with their tales of questionable wealth and fame seem designed purely to irritate those of us who are just trying to muddle through each day's trials and tribulations as best we can. Over time it has become ridiculous, to the point where we're now bombarded with relatively unexceptional people doing quite obviously unexceptional things. (I present the 'celebrity selfie' as the prosecution's first piece of evidence). I know some people revel in it, in much the same way as medieval proletariats revelled in every action of a king or queen, but I think it has become an unhealthy state of affairs.

At the same time, we seem to have become a race that almost celebrates disaster on both personal and grand scales: the reality TV show contestant with some terrible back story; the shelves of supposedly autobiographical fiction with tales of childhood woe and despair; the television news cameras that have to be in the faces of people experiencing fresh trauma. Most worryingly, we've got to the stage where to be normal — and especially normal and happy — is almost seen as a lack of awareness, experience or aspiration.

In some small way, I wanted this book to be an antidote to all that. We're two relatively normal blokes, with a relatively normal father/son relationship, who have had relatively normal lives. Even this bike ride across France, while perhaps seeming extreme to some, can be accomplished quite happily by any other relatively healthy, normal person. We certainly understand the world can be a difficult place — we've seen it at first hand just like everybody else — but life always goes on and there's a better moment just round the corner. Trust me, I found myself having to say that for the best part of 600 miles.

So as you read our story we hope you'll think about the book inside you; the things you're proud of; the life you're leading. We also hope *Rides of Passage* might inspire some people to jump on their bikes.

I couldn't possibly say if I'd recommend cycling across France, though.

Matt Lamy, March 2016

The Riders

Matt Lamy

After an inauspicious start that saw him chucking his guts up at the side of a dual-carriageway outside of Saint Malo, taking a desperate poo in a field near Saint Médard, then being crippled with back pain, it took a few days and a lot of Tiger Balm before things improved for 15-year-old Matt back in 1994. Thankfully, the lure of cheese, bread and cider each night got him through.

Against expectations, that first trans-France bike tour didn't put him off cycling for life and Matt went on to become one of Britain's top cycling magazine journalists. He has been a staff member of *Cycling Weekly*, *Cycle Sport* and *Mountain Bike Rider*, as well as being chief writer of *Cycling Active* from its launch until 2015. Matt has also been editor of *What Cycle?* and *Fit2Ride* magazines and was named IPC Media Specialist Writer of the Year in 2011 and 2013. He is also author of two books: *Lance and Le Tour* and the peerless *100 Strangest Unexplained Mysteries*.

Now a very tired 37 year old, Matt lives in Coulsdon, Surrey with his wife Manda and their eight-year-old twin sons. Did he fare any better during the 2015 ride? Read on...

Introduction

Arthur Lamy

Known to his family as 'The Old Chap' and to his grandchildren as 'Papa Arf', Arthur wholeheartedly accepted the challenge as main guide, back-rubber and wheel-spoke-replacer for the original 1994 cycle tour. Thankfully, his occupation as a cycle shop manager meant that patiently dealing with an awkward berk on a bike came as second nature.

In 2010, after 28 years in the cycle trade, Arthur decided to have a change of profession and has become one of Jersey's foremost tourist guides. You may have seen him on such things as the back page of the *Sunday Times* travel section, BBC2's *Holiday of My Lifetime*, or caught a fleeting glimpse of his dashing Tilley-hat-wearing bonce on the 'Visit Jersey' advert during a commercial break in *Coronation Street*.

Arthur is an award-winning photographer and has written for a range of national magazines. He is also the author of *Jersey Cycles* and *St Helier: A History and Celebration.* As something of a local media personality, in 2013 he took part in BBC Jersey's version of *Strictly Come Dancing for Comic Relief.* His 'paso' really was something to behold.

Now a sprightly 63, Arthur has three grandchildren and lives in Jersey with his wife of 39 years, Susan.

Note for readers

Each chapter starts with Matt and Arthur's original diary entries that correspond with the equivalent day of the modern journey. For the main body of the text, Matt and Arthur's narratives are interwoven: Matt's words are all in an upright font, Arthur's words are in italics.

Rides of Passage has been written first and foremost as a story to be enjoyed. However, you can find more detailed information about Matt and Arthur's 2015 ride; see maps of the exact the route they took each day; read about the equipment they used; and view photos of their bikes at **www.ridesofpassage.info.**

RIDES OF PASSAGE

DAY 1
Leaving Home

Sunday August 14, 1994 — Saint Malo to Saint Médard sur Ille (44.5 miles)
Sunday August 2, 2015 — Saint Malo to Saint Aubin du Cormier (47.4 miles)

Matt aged 15

After waking up flipping early - Dad had been up for ages - I got dressed and loaded my bags on the bike. I could hardly lift the back of my bike off the floor. Dad had a quick cup of tea and we set off after saying goodbye to everybody.

We rode the bikes down to the harbour and checked-in. Uncle Ernie came to see us off, as did Aunty Jane, although she was quite late. Then we got in the queue and met two blokes who knew Dad and who were also going to France to cycle tour. Dad chatted to them and we got on the boat.

The boat trip over was not very good for me as I didn't feel that well. The boat was rocking all over the place.

We arrived in Saint Malo on time and cycled through the suburbs of Saint Malo trying to get on the right road for Rennes. Luckily I knew the area near this road from a school rugby trip, but we still went straight past it. I told Dad I thought we were going the wrong way, so he asked a man in French which direction to take.

While going along the correct road, which happened to be a motorway, I felt really ill so we stopped and I was sick. After a while I was alright again. Eventually we turned off onto a load of little roads to get to Combourg. On the way we had one woman cheering us on.

In Combourg we sat down at a pub and had a drink of water, which cost us 34 francs. A bit further down the road a group of kids came out to see us and ask us if we wanted a drink. Dad said we had just had one, which was to prove stupid.

By this time I was really struggling. I needed breaks all the time and had to push my bike up hills. By the time we saw a sign for Montreuil I was dying, so Dad decided to head for the next campsite at Saint Médard, supposedly 2km away. It ended up being 5km away. I desperately needed the toilet, so I went in a field with Aunty Jane's soft, moist toilet tissue and did it there.

The campsite was not far away in the little village of Saint Médard. However, when we arrived no one was there. We set everything up and went to look for something to eat. Nothing was open except for a small bar, so we went in and had two beers and two packets of chocolate biscuits. This pub was very French with only five of us in there to start. It gradually filled up so we went back to the tent and looked at the maps.

We plan that tomorrow we will wake up early and try to miss out Rennes completely. Our route should be 105km.

We went to sleep at 9pm. We also found out the camera battery is dead so can't take pictures.

Today, taking into account leaving the house, we travelled 71.6km.

Arthur aged 42

Hard day in the saddle for both me and Matt. Matt was unwell on the boat and this carried over a bit when we actually got going. The roads seem to go on forever, especially the one that we took first, which was an 'N' road. The first few miles of having cars pass you at 50 or 60mph is very encouraging because it makes you go faster. It must be said that they also give you a wide berth.

We were getting tired and despondent after Combourg. After struggling through Dinge and Gripel we decided to go on to any campsite we could find. The sign for Saint Médard looked promising with its picture of caravans and tents. Alas, we nearly rode past it as it was only a field with small washing facilities. In my honesty, I tried all over the place to pay for our pitch, but the 'Marie' where you sign in was shut, as was the restaurant 'en face'.

I was starving and Matt was resting his body after two trips to the loo, one al fresco, one in the salubrious campsite facilities. The kids I spoke to outside the Marie offered me an acorn to eat, but after I refused it they thought that I could have it anyway and winged it at me as I rode off. One young lady also pulled me up on my masculine and feminine nouns.

After pitching the tent we made another sortie for food. We again met my authoritative madam and her friends. Again they informed me that everything was shut and that Saint Médard sur Ille was dead on Sundays. They very kindly advised me that there was water in the taps at the toilets of the Marie, and sent an untalkative lad of about eight to escort us there and check we drunk it.

On our return Matt spotted the open door of a bar and we eagerly went into feast ourselves on whatever it contained. Two halves of lager and their entire stock of chocolate biscuits later, we emerged ready for sleep.

Highlights of the day:
— Met two customers. One had a broken spoke.
— The camping at Saint Médard was a field with toilets.
— Camera battery failed.
— Couldn't find a phone to call home.

Matt aged 36

So the old chap and I are back on the road, back in the saddle, back riding across a country that seems so familiar — growing up in Jersey I could literally see the French coast across the water most days — yet so very different once you step off the ferry in Saint Malo.

In theory we should be way more prepared than last time. Rather than a schoolboy I'm now a professional cycling journalist and have been for almost 15 years. Dad's a tourist guide who spends most days on his feet or in the saddle, so although he's older he should be just as fit as he was 21 years ago. We've got mobile phones with all sorts of functions and information available to us, not to mention the ability to call home whenever we need extra help. Our kit is all good stuff, and we've spent months thinking about this trip. Rather like last time, though, there's been a conspicuous lack of dedicated 'training' by either of us. Old habits die hard.

In 1994 we literally did just set off, hoping for the best, with a bag of Michelin maps and a vague plan to find some pay phones en route. As it turned out, back then I don't think we actually managed to call home for the first three days. My wife and boys would have kittens if that situation was to play out now.

And I suppose that's the biggest difference for me on this trip. Aged 15 I was far from being a hero when it came to leaving home but I went on sports trips and cadet trips with school, and I was taking at least one large part of home — dad — with me on that epic bike journey. Things have changed a lot since then. I haven't lived in Jersey with mum and dad since I was 19, and home now consists of my wife Manda and my seven-year-old twin boys Adam and David.

That meant leaving this morning was more of a protracted chore than last time. Manda and the boys wanted to take photos of dad and me, and then come down to the boat to wave us off. I probably would have been happier with a quicker and more painless farewell, but then it wouldn't have been fair on them. The boys are going to be without daddy for the best part of a fortnight; in the years since they were born I've only ever spent one night away from them.

Arthur aged 63

Hindsight is a great thing, and sometimes I even take some notice of what has gone before. So with all the knowledge gleaned from a trip 21 years ago, I made a mental note to prepare well ahead this time.

In fact, in many ways the preparation and thought that goes before it is almost as attractive as the journey itself. So I felt that we could improve on what we did last time, given that we had plenty of notice to get everything ready. I did give the trip a great deal of thought, and as usual did not do much. But I did purchase several vital items of kit, such as mesh bags for clothing, extra locks and enormous bottle cages to carry the huge bottles of water that are essential to our ride.

I really felt that I had spent a generous amount of time on preparation. Certainly it was more than the last time, which now, all these years later, seems like we decided to do it on one day and then set off on the boat the next. Of course, we were both card-carrying members of the Cyclists Touring Club (now known as Cycling UK), but other than that we had actually very little cycle touring experience.

We left the house this morning in a flurry of photo calls, not from the local media but from Matt's wife, Amanda and his twins. We are going cycling in France, not the moon, but the urgency to record our wobbly progress up and down the road outside Lamy Towers did remind us that this was not an everyday event and inevitably brought home the magnitude of our trip. My bike and bags tipped the scales at just over six stone. This is half my own bodyweight.

We cycled down to Saint Helier and lined up in the queue to board the ferry, trying to look as nonchalant as possible as if this was something that we had done hundreds of times before, not just once.

I just about manage to man up and hold back the strange swell of emotion that tickles behind the eyes and nose at moments like this, so dad and I wave to Manda and the boys, and make it through to the loading ramp of the ferry without any great scenes of uncontrolled sentiment.

To be honest, I've been through worse in the 21 years since we last set off on this voyage. The evening of my 19th birthday was spent on the phone to mum, teary, hundreds of miles from home in a city I had never visited before, alone in an uninhabited halls of residence with only the distant sound of dripping taps for company.

Earlier that day, as the taxi from East Midlands airport crested the trunk road into Sheffield, I had seen the strangely magical vista of the city's steel and concrete jungle broadly sweep ahead of me. Sheffield would be my new university home.

Having grown up in an island nine miles by five miles, it was like nothing I had ever seen before and the untold opportunities that lay among the streets and buildings ahead was massively exciting. Unfortunately the excitement died away later that evening when, after enjoying a kebab and stroll around a deserted university, I realised this was no daytrip — I really was on my own.

Funnily enough, another memory I have from that particular day is being at Jersey airport ready to board the flight. My best mates and Manda — we've known each other since we were 17 — came to wave me away. However, it was dad who dropped me off. He came in to the departure hall but didn't hang about; I think the emotion of the moment got to him. I've never seen the old chap cry, that was about the closest it's got.

Like most people's life stories, everything worked out OK in the end. I had four incredible, responsibility-free years in Sheffield. And it was the start of the long journey of becoming a grown-up.

At least our trip across France will be over in a fortnight. I hope.

So dad and I shouldn't feel too overawed about what we're about to do. But I'm not blind to the difficult tasks that may face us in the days ahead. For example, dad has his moments where he's a trifle distracted or, in the parlance of the modern cliché, he's 'singing from a different hymn sheet'. Last night was a case in point. Looking at the weather forecast for today, which predicted temperatures of 30 degrees Celsius in Saint Malo, I said: "It's going to be super hot tomorrow, let's not go too hard and perhaps aim to finish a little earlier than our route plan says."

To which the old fella replied, quite seriously: "Yes, let's try to go beyond the schedule and get ahead of the game."

Thankfully there were witnesses who all fell about laughing at the incongruity of that little conversation, and who no doubt silently wished me luck over the next two weeks.

I don't know if my contrived nonchalance is in any way apparent, but I must be one of the least-travelled people in the world. I have plans, but like bike tour preparations, these are often more comfortable (and less expensive) than actually going somewhere.

My wife Susan and I nearly moved to Southampton in our early twenties. Sue had a place at university to study accountancy, and I, as the faithful boyfriend was going along too. In fact, my boss at the time had even found me employment at a screenprinters across Southampton Water. With the usual absence of preplanning, we booked a hotel and a plane, and left the rest to chance. So although my in-laws thought Sue would be better off without me — yes, completely correct — we would have gone together. On the Friday night, before the Saturday morning departure, Sue changed her mind and we stayed in Jersey.

I think that this decision was generally popular with everyone, although there were no obvious signs of jubilation. Our lives returned to normal and chugged along as before. Rather a pity in some ways, as being jettisoned into somewhere completely different and having to stand on your own two feet must ultimately be beneficial.

So when Matt went off to university, and in due course his younger brother Richard as well, I felt it was a very good thing. Naturally, as a parent it was painful and unnerving to see them go, but unlike the upbringing that Sue and I had, where parents came first and usually got what they wanted, we felt that we should set our kids free and see what they could make of the world.

So where have I actually been? One trip I took alone was to Grenoble in the French Alps. At the time, I managed a cycle shop that sold Peugeot bicycles and I was keen to cement and grow links with them. So off I went on a late flight to Gatwick to stay at a B&B overnight, and leave the following day on the charter to Grenoble. With my leather Filofax, my suit, my shiny shoes, and my Donald Trump book on world domination, I felt I was the man.

I didn't feel quite so much the man three days later as the charter aircraft on which I was returning to Gatwick landed late, and I ended up watching the little monorail that goes between North and South Terminals disappear in the distance, along with any hope of catching my plane home to Jersey. But I came home the next day, Peugeot picked up the cost of my adventures, and life went on. So here I am 21 years after our first ride across France definitely older, very arguably wiser, but not that much more travelled.

Matt and I take positions at the ramp onto the ferry. Bicycles and motorbikes have precedence over the cars and we line up ahead of them; not because we are so superior, more like they don't want us gassed by all the carbon monoxide that the vehicles are putting out. As expected, someone I know creeps past coming off the ferry and says hello, asking where we are going. They say that they have just come from the South of France and tell us that it is hotter than usual there. It's not really the news we want to hear.

Within minutes we are called and, as instructed, walk our bikes down the gangway and onto the ship. There's no need to elasticate the bikes to the superstructure, says a crew member, so we join both bikes together with bungees in the hope that they will not move around too much during the voyage. Then we head upstairs onto the open deck to wave goodbye and take a few images of Jersey as it slips into the distance.

Now we're on our way, on board the ferry watching our island motherland disappear in the distance. It's not long before the shores of our Gallic forefathers — a family history that I'm sure dad will tell every French person with whom we come into contact — appears on the horizon. Soon we are docked and allowed to get off the boat.

The first job to do on this trip is to get our GPS devices working. Unlike

1994 we have all sorts of technology at our disposal, and the ability to track and record our course is one of them. Had we thought about it, we could probably have set up a SatNav function on my phone to guide us as well, but that wouldn't have been anywhere near as much fun, even if it would stop us taking a wrong turn little more than a few hundred yards from the ferry terminal. Somehow we end up in the very picturesque but very wrong Cité peninsular. The first step on any journey is always the trickiest, and it takes a little while to get our bearings and a fully functional sense of correlation between distances on the map and real distances on the road.

Eventually, though, we find a road heading south. Our route notes are taken from a slightly updated version of our 1994 trip and they explain that the option we originally took away from Saint Malo — an 'N' road — is no longer viable. Now I'm a little more used to major roads in Britain, I wonder if it was really a viable option even back then. In any case, ready to prevent an early cock-up, over the last couple of days I've researched an alternative way to avoid this initial hurdle and get on track.

We follow the kinds of roads that you would find on the outskirts of any large town or city, darting from roundabout to roundabout, weaving through hypermarkets, car dealerships and home improvement megastores. It's a Sunday so they're all shut — France obviously hasn't changed that much in 21 years.

Gradually urban life starts to fade away and we are out among fields, cruising between villages and pockets of civilisation. Every now and then we see posters at the roadside for a local music event, with a full-frame picture of the headlining artiste. I won't name him for fear of being sued, but he looks uniquely French and rather like the sort of gone-to-seed celebrity who could be part of an historical abuse investigation were he a famous personality in Britain.

We climb a small crest and from the top a vast blanket of rural northern France stretches out ahead of us. "Voila Papa, c'est la France," I shout, but the old fella seems intent on going as hard and as fast as he can today, stopping occasionally only to record notes into his dictaphone or take out his camera.

And what of the weather? As promised, it is indeed super hot, so drink stops are relatively frequent and we even reapply sunspray at one point. At this stage it's all rather pleasant as we keep to minor roads, navigating from hamlet to hamlet. It's only when we rejoin our official route, on the far more substantial D73, that the going starts to get tough. The road is long, straight, and comes with an added ingredient: a relentless northerly wind blowing in our faces.

It really is hard going, but at least it's powering dad's windmill. We have a few options for recharging our electrical equipment on this trip. I have a Tigra dynamo that sits on the outside of the front wheel hub and which can recharge a good proportion of my iPhone. I also have a small solar panel system, which one of my friends lent me as a back-up. Dad, meanwhile, has a little windmill that powers an internal battery, which can then be used to partially recharge his phone. Before the trip there was some discussion about where the best place to situate this windmill might be. Mum, ever on the case to rib the old boy, suggested behind his saddle might be most effective. The handlebar won out and in these conditions it's been spinning tremendously — I doubt that, even after a fulsome meal of bean crock, dad would be better able to power it himself.

For all my lack of overseas experience, this isn't the first time I've written about cycling in France. In recent years, I have been lucky enough to write one or two travel articles, even one with Matt to promote Cycle West: a set of routes through the south of England, the north of France and Jersey. The piece was to go in a cycling magazine that Matt worked for and the Jersey tourism brochure Pure Jersey. *The piece ended up being called 'Double Lamy' and it entailed Matt riding and describing the way from Corfe Castle to Weymouth, with me cycling and describing the route from Mont Saint Michel to Saint Malo. Then we symbolically met up at the Jersey ferry terminal and cycled around the island together.*

To do my section, I decided to stay over near Mont Saint Michel and cycle back the next day. It's probably possible for a young scorcher on a carbon racing bike to go there and back in a day without staying a night. But I do very little scorching these days, and experience has taught me that you discover a lot more if you proceed at a steady pace.

While I was near Mont Saint Michel, my dear family were concerned about me. I had neither contacted them, nor were they able to reach me, and understandably they feared that I might be lodged in the grill of an 18-wheeler heading for Montpellier. Foolishly, I had not left any address for my hotel, so they were very much in the dark.

Now, I have to admit that I cannot go much more than 12 hours without talking to my wife, and I too was keen to phone home. In the past all my previous phones roamed automatically, so there I was desperately changing my position hoping to find a signal. That was until I realised that I had to switch roaming on and choose a provider. Knowing all this, on this latest jaunt I have already switched to roaming and chosen a provider. However, now we are in France it seems I cannot phone home, although they can phone me. But I can send texts. Hmm.

To be honest, there's not much capacity for calling. We're finding the going much harder than expected. The temperature is well over 30 degrees and it feels like we have a headwind most of the way. The scenery is pleasant, though, with hay and sunflowers and the odd heron flying beside as we wheel along.

After a while we reach Combourg and, in theory, should be retracing our tyre treads from 1994. To be honest, neither of us recognises a thing. The town itself is like a potted history of Tour de France team sponsors with branches of Caisse d'Epargne, Crédit Agricole and FDJ. We stop for a drink and a biscuit — I brought some emergency supplies, fearing a repeat of the national Sunday curfew we encountered last time — then set back off on our 'D' road, with the next stop at Sens de Bretagne.

As well as the boring, long straight roads, the depressing headwind, and the 30-degree heat, we find an extra detail to spice things up — wave after wave of interminably rolling little hills. They're not enough to make you feel like you've taken on a real climb, but with bikes weighing five or six stone — 30kg — these hillocks put us into a routine of slowly going up, then slowly coming down, one after the other. Truly, the sight of them emerging from the horizon is incredibly soul-sapping. How long have we been off the boat already?

Thankfully, to either side there are more interesting, sweeping vistas of red and yellow fields. But under that sun we are already feeling enough physical pressure to be unable to appreciate them. In any case, while I enjoy looking at the scenery, I have embarrassingly little clue about flora and fauna. I prefer people and ideas and even machines. My attitude to the scenery and splendour of the natural world is very much like my attitude, as a happily married man, to the sight of pretty ladies. I'm delighted to gaze upon them, but I have no intention to become intimately acquainted, let alone go rummaging in the undergrowth.

That said, we are forced to take shelter in the shade wherever we can. I make sure to drink lots of water. Dad should probably be drinking more, although he did at least accept the newfangled sorcery of an electrolyte tab.

We stop outside an old folks' home at La Tronchet for a drink and whatever Matt has brought with him. This turns out to be hydration tablets to add to our water, some chocolate muesli bars and a biscuit-flavoured jam that we squeeze out of a sachet. It's all essential stuff for the modern road cyclist, so I'm led to believe.

Day 1 — Leaving Home

While both of us are slightly more worldly-wise than last time we did this trip, as men who were born in a small bit of land floating in the Channel, I think we'll always feel an internal battle against some kind of inherent bumpkin-ism. Jersey isn't quite the backwater people imagine, and I've comfortably lived in urban areas of mainland Britain for almost as long as I spent at home, but I know there are some experiences that are still alien to me.

For example, the first time I'd had a sit-down Chinese meal rather than a takeaway was for Manda's 21st birthday. I'd only ever seen hot towels delivered with tongs on an aeroplane before. So when I was handed one after the starters I gave my hands a good wipe. It was then that I was told they were actually the pancakes to go with the hoi sin duck. The second time I took Manda for a Chinese meal it was a romantic affair, with candle-lit tables. I looked at the menu, decided what I wanted, then noticed our candle had somehow been extinguished. Unfortunately, I then realised the back of my menu was fully aflame.

I have no intention to go cycle touring across China.

We soldier on with an idea that Sens de Bretagne with its campsite will be our salvation. Sadly, it appears that Sens has lost its campsite, despite signs all around. Over a tall garden wall, I speak to a woman pegging out her washing. She tells me that the campsite has been closed for years. However, I did notice that she offered chambres d'hôte, so perhaps she has an agenda?

By now all supplies are diminishing, so we decide to press on to the next campsite location — Saint Aubin du Cormier — where apparently there are two campsites. Hallelujah! As we are exhausted and everything is shut on Sunday (and very possibly every other day of the week around here), we really have little choice but to keep going.

Ever the paranoiac, once we've left the old lady in Sens de Bretagne behind, the old chap suggests she must have some rooms to rent and was just trying to put us off camping. I'm not convinced.

I'm also not thrilled at having to cycle another 12km, but after a succession of more rundown and shuttered villages we make it to Saint Aubin du Cormier. The municipal campsite is easy to find and dad does the signing-in duties. We are already a little further ahead of Saint Médard where we camped back in 1994, so morale is high. I'm actually a little annoyed we didn't pass through Saint Médard on this trip. Seeing how sleepy these French rural outcrops are, I have a suspicion that right in the middle of the village they may have a 21-year-old statue of a middle-aged man and his teenage son on their bikes, dedicated to the 'Unknown Cycle Tourists'. Now I will never know.

Dad tries to find out if anywhere is open for food or drink. As I'm the only one actually carrying any water — dad fitted an extra-large bottle cage to his bike before we set off, but for some reason didn't see fit to place an extra-large bottle holding any water in the cage (don't ask) — water supplies are ultra low. "Non, monsieur," says the charming lady in the campsite office. "C'est la dimanche!"

Ah yes, that old chestnut — it's Sunday. I've spent the last 20 miles dreaming of a cold Coke, but never mind. Still, if a giant asteroid ever hits Earth on the sabbath, France is assured to escape devastation: "C'est la dimanche," seems a powerful enough excuse to avert even armageddon.

I have to quell my frustration because a very pleasant chap staying at the campsite comes over for a chat, intrigued by dad's windmill. As expected, dad gives him the old: "My mother's family were from Brittany, my father's family were from Normandy" spiel. Finally we can head to our pitch, which is in an elevated field, totally to ourselves, but accessible only by a flight of steps. All very pretty with a view over the nearby lake, but a giant pain in the arse with machines weighing five stone. We have to unload our bags and carry them and the bikes up separately.

After putting up the tent, dad says he has no time for a shower, he wants a cold drink. It's no surprise: he hasn't drunk enough today. We walk into the village looking for a bar. Truly it seems as if nothing is open, although the impressive bell tower in the local church is working well enough. Then we stumble upon a hole-in-the-wall takeaway pizza place. Even better, their fridge is stocked with huge bottles of Liptons Ice Tea, soft drinks and Raison Loic cider. We load up with two bottles of non-alcoholic drink, two bottles of cider and a huge pizza — neither of us really cares what is on it.

The cycle touring gods are smiling on us. And so much for the: "Ah non, monsieur — c'est la dimanche."

We have the entire 'tent' area to ourselves; the majority of campsite clients seemed to be caravans or mobile homes. After sprawling on our backs to regain our strength after carrying the bikes and bags up, we put up the tent, and consolidate our belongings. Matt thinks that I have an abnormal fear of being robbed — he's probably right.

One thing I have learnt very quickly on this trip is that I will never starve with Matt by my side. A brief stroll around the ghost town that is Saint Aubin du Cormier on Sunday reveals an open pizza parlour. We order a 40cm 'Country' pizza, then return to our pitch and refuel. It's pretty idyllic, with a great view over the lake and the noise of pentanque players nearby, even if one does sound like Barbara Windsor when she laughs.

Day 1 — Leaving Home

After what amounts to truly slap-up cycle-touring nosh, we use the rather impressive site facilities to wash our day's riding clothes and have a shower. I also try to rectify or at least nullify what may well prove to be my biggest error on this trip. I have fitted a brand new Brooks saddle to my bike and it's already starting to cause me — in the words of Frank Spencer — 'a bit of trouble'. Brooks may produce the finest saddles known to man but they're made of leather and take a few hundred miles to break in, shaping to the contours of your bum. Until that happens, they're über hard.

We phone home and I chat to Manda and the boys. I'm very tired but the bikes have held up well — not a given considering the immense weight they are carrying — and at least we've made a start. I look at the map and plan tomorrow's route.

It's 9.30pm and it's still hot.

I eat Matt's Kendal mint cake for dessert, and once in my sleeping bag, I soon plummet into a deep sleep.

RIDES OF PASSAGE

DAY 2
Our Work Begins

Monday August 15, 1994 —Saint Médard sur Ille to Saint Julien (64 miles)
Monday August 3, 2015 — Saint Aubin du Cormier to Vern d'Anjou (61.2 miles)

Matt aged 15

We set off bright 'n' early at about 7.30am. We had planned to leave earlier but discovered that it was still dark at 6am. I had a bad night's sleep, with people outside shouting until 10pm.

Unfortunately we discovered that it had either rained or there was dew, so everything outside and the tent itself was soaked. After packing up our stuff while everybody was asleep, we headed for Saint Aubin. We reached this quickly and then continued to Liffré. Here we bought a load of 'pains au chocolat' and some drinks. I didn't feel too well but we continued.

We next got to the point where we would cross the motorway leading to Rennes. Here we got slightly lost, ending up in Noyel. While here Dad tried to ring Mum but couldn't get through.

We continued on our way to Châteaugiront and then Janzé. While here, we realised French shops are shut on a Monday as well as Sunday, so it was a stroke of luck getting our food this morning. In Janzé Dad tried to ring Mum but couldn't get through. We took our helmets off after leaving the town.

Our next stop ended up being a little village called La Couyère. We were not supposed to go there but it was another stroke of luck. In La Couyère there was a bar tabac that Dad went into to try and get some food. In this bar he managed to buy some cheese, a bottle of wine and two bottles of water. Dad tried to ring Mum again. We later realised we were using the wrong phone code.

We got an ice-cream and some drinks in Châteaubriant before aiming for Saint Julien, 12km down the road. By now I was struggling and the sun was boiling. We reached the town and went straight on through, aiming to camp at the next campsite we could find.

We followed the signs for a campsite to a small farm. Dad went and talked to the man in charge while I recuperated. The guy was a complete prat but friendly and from England. After setting up our stuff he said we could have a cup of tea. It seems he owns the place and lives here with his wife. He was about 65 and as interesting as Mr Bean.

We had a cup of tea with the man, although he jumped up startled when a cat stroked his leg and sent the tea all over us. Then we washed our clothes and hung them to dry. I had a shower using cold water and we had dinner. This was half a baguette with cheese and wine. Much better than last night.

Afterwards, the guy, whose name was Graham brought a table up for us. It was just an excuse for him to tell us his life history. In the campsite there is nobody else at all. Dad went for a wash and we got our stuff sorted.

Today we did 101.6km, about 10km more than we should have but we still ended up 14km from our objective, Candé. However, I felt much better today and hopefully we can catch up tomorrow. Hopefully tomorrow the shops will be open as well.

Arthur aged 42

Easier day today. Hills seem flatter, obviously we are getting fitter, and we did the first few miles with a very cool morning mist enveloping the countryside as we went along. This enabled us to cover quite a good distance without noticing it.

At Liffré, we found a boulangerie open. I bought six chocolate croissants and a baguette. I was impressed that I could choose my baguette. I also bought two Cokes and two other soft drinks from a very pleasant woman who spoke to us.

We made good speed onwards. Alas, being Monday, mostly everything was shut. I tried to telephone home several times but when I finally worked out the correct sequence of numbers, I could not find a phone box.

We stopped a lot more regularly and voluntarily than yesterday, and this seems to make the distance slightly more bearable. Once past noon, though, the whole body starts to tire and the excessive heat did little to help us those few further kilometres.

We bought provisions at La Couyère: Laughing Cow cheese, a bottle of Bergerac and three litres of Vittell water. The last item being the thread on which the whole expedition now hinges.

Matt was tiring this afternoon, so it was full speed ahead for 'Le Camping', and I spotted a sign by the roadside. We pursued its directions and found ourselves on a camping 'à la ferme', (ie, few facilities). A very nice Englishman welcomed us and gave us a cup of tea, and nearly his life story.

Highlights of the day:

— I had a shave and a shower. Very little water came out of the showerhead.

— I did the laundry and hung it out on an interesting selection of lines.

Matt aged 36

Jesus Christ! I had to invoke His name quite literary this morning when a litany of church bells loudly rang out at seven o'clock. That must be the time people get up round these parts. There is something oddly dictatorial, almost *1984*-like about a whole village being commanded to get up as one by some unseen force. The even weirder thing was that the bells went off again rather haphazardly five minutes later. I can only presume God had hit the snooze button.

I didn't sleep very well last night. We had the inner tent doors open for cool air, but the outer doors resolutely closed for the old chap's security. However, sometime in the depths of darkness I felt something substantial crawl onto my foot, so I decided to close the inner tent door, too.

A bigger problem was that for most of the night I could feel my heart racing and beating in my ears. I did what any self-respecting hypochondriac would do and took my heart rate. It was about 90bpm, which is pretty much double my normal resting rate.

'Whoah,' I imagine you're thinking. 'How does a fat lad like you have such a low heart rate? Truly cycling must help with baseline fitness.' Actually no, it's got nothing to do with cycling. I do credit one sport for my low heart rate, but it's absolutely the most inactive of all competitive activities. For three years I was a member of the UK Cadet full-bore rifle shooting team (at Bisley in 1995 I came second in the national Young Rifleman of the Year competition). I don't shoot anymore — and when I did it was only at large paper or plastic targets, nothing sweet and/or furry — but the remnants of technique and training from that period have stuck with me.

To be a successful shot you need as steady a hand and as low a heart rate as possible. I've even heard stories about Russian snipers being able to squeeze the trigger in between heartbeats. I can normally drop my heart rate below 45bpm to order. But last night I really couldn't, no matter what. Probably the 30-degree heat and that 1.5-litre bottle of Lipton's Ice Tea I downed with our pizza had something to do with it. Incidentally, what happened to the uneaten slices of pizza? Dad told me a story about how some ne'er-do-well bike rep he used to know who would eat leftover takeaway pizza the next morning — imagine that! — and so the old fella chucked ours away last night. Welcome to the generation gap. Nevermind, I'm sure we'll be inundated with eating opportunities today...

So our first full day on the bikes beckons. We get up, do our morning ablutions, pack the tent, then have to manhandle all our kit down those blasted steps to head away. A new 'chef de campsite' is already cleaning the showers at 8.30am as we leave. He seems to think we haven't paid, so dad has to whip out his receipt. I'm starting to suspect the old chap's inherent paranoia comes from his fabled French heritage.

Arthur aged 63

We never noticed that the church bell in Saint Aubin was turned off during the night until it struck up at 07.00hrs this morning, and again a few minutes later, just to make sure we hadn't missed it the first time. This manages to wake us and we fumble about a bit, but eventually get up. So begins the routine that we will no doubt perfect by the end of the trip, namely 'taking the tent down'.

Matt has bought a new three-man tent for this adventure and, as well as being sufficiently roomy, it needs very little work to put up and take down. Three poles are enough to hold it up and make a small porch, with maybe eight guy lines doing everything else. It takes only a few minutes to put away. The biggest problem is the enormous amount of condensation that accumulates inside the flysheet.

I try drying it with my special travel towel, a bit of kit I have bought especially for this trip. Packing up not much bigger than a hankie, this hi-tech cloth can wick away incredible amounts of moisture. It does have a couple of drawbacks, though. One is that it has the texture of a chamois leather, which is fine for people with some kind of motoring fetish. The second is that its diminutive proportions mean you can't wrap it round you as you saunter back from the shower. Well, not without something dangling in full view. And we aren't planning to stay at those kinds of campsites.

With the tent down, we repack our bags and get ready to move. Even in the remotest of landscapes, I'm always afraid that someone will steal my possessions. Yes., I agree this is completely without foundation, but I would say in my defence, I spent 30 years in retailing and it's amazing what people will nick. Because of this I'm super cautious and I put all my bags inside the tent porch, and furthermore, I also like to have it securely zipped up at night. My dear wife Susan told Matt that I might appear slightly odd at times during the trip, and this is one of those times. I'm sure that there will be many others that will reveal themselves in the days to come, and probably resurface in a light-hearted fashion over the family dinner table long after.

All set to go, and another careful descent of the stone steps down from the 'tent area avec une belle vue du lac', to ground level. Both Matt and I wear cycling shoes with inset cleats. This allows you to walk, to a certain extent, and to clip into the pedals as well. The cleats clatter on the stone steps and threaten to slip off at any second, but we concentrate and make several trips with bikes and bags.

My concentration must be excellent because on one of these trips I manage to cut my head on a branch and I only realise it a little while later when Matt asks me what the black stuff on my head is. It turns out to be dried blood. A hearty application of a wet wipe or two soon has me looking normal again.

Unlike the last time we cycled across France, when the most technical thing we had was a cycle computer, this time we have brought a relatively comprehensive range of gadgets to note distance, altitude, and even make a map as we ride along. Before we left Jersey we felt confident that we could generate sufficient power to keep all these things working. However, the first sign of a problem comes before we have even left Saint Aubin. Not only do I have to put another set of batteries into my GPS, but I also notice that it is already 18 per cent full. That suggests that I won't be able to record the whole 10-day trip.

We set off and Englishness creeps in as Matt cycles up the road on the left-hand side. I remind him where he is.

It takes a little while to orientate ourselves again as we leave Saint Aubin but soon we are on another 'D' road heading through a succession of little towns. The heat of yesterday has dissipated, at least for a while (I used a weather app on my phone last night and know this won't last), and the sky is overcast.

I may struggle to remember the villages' names the minute we pass through them, but it's far harder to forget some of the incredible churches we're spotting en route. The designs are varied and amazing, from the cupola and steeple combo in Livré sur Changeon to the colourful and ornate creation halfway down the incline in Val d'Izé. Every collection of dwellings, no matter how small, seems to have it's own mini — or not so mini — cathedral. Christianity is certainly alive in these parts, even if Christians or indeed people of any denomination seem few and far between. The bleak, grey dourness of these villages can be oddly beautiful in the gloomy early morning, but we see little life.

One person we do spot meandering along the roadside is a wiry, toothless old fellow in dirty clothes and flat cap. In many ways he reminds me very much of my grandfather, dad's dad. If that's the French heritage dad speaks of, I'm glad mum's genetics seem to be winning the battle for my DNA.

We make good if not particularly enjoyable time, again following big 'D' roads, which continue with their pattern of long straights made notable only for rows of humps, like waves coming in to shore. A routine develops of heading down one trough at 20mph, then struggling up the other side at 8mph.

Dad is going well spinning a light gear — rather like he who shall not be named (Lance Armstrong) used to do. In fact, technically dad is doping, too, as a heel injury means he is on prescription painkillers. I must check he has a valid Therapeutic Use Exemption form for them. Meanwhile, I'm rather more like Jan

Ullrich: I've been metaphorically eating pies until just before the big event and now I'm desperately trying to burn them off.

I've heard people say, on more than one occasion, that I don't look like a cyclist. True, the last person to say it barely looked human himself and was yet to fully understand the wonder of fire, but his critique is something I can't really deny. Cyclists, as the stereotype would have us believe — and as a surprising number of cyclists seem happy to conform to — are all rake thin and either look like little boys, or have beards, or are bald with beards. I, on the other hand, am 16 stone and carry more weight above my waist than below it. My beard comes and goes depending only on my idleness, and until I could deny my genetics no longer, for most of my adult life I've had very long hair.

Not all cyclists should feel they have to look like a waif. Medical science might be an ever-evolving sector but I think it's fair to say that there is a well-established theory that fit people who have a bit of timber on them can cope with long-term illness better. If I remember rightly, some recent research I read suggested that bigger people are more likely to survive heart attacks than skinnies. Of course, there are no doubt caveats to all this, but essentially thin doesn't necessarily mean fit.

Of course, you might have become a cyclist specifically to achieve the body beautiful. Boy, are you barking up the wrong tree. Have you seen a pro rider's physique? When Michelangelo was sculpting David he didn't opt for a pigeon-chested, stick-armed sapling. Maybe you're on your bike to get back in those skinny jeans you used to have. Sadly you'll probably never know if you've reduced your waist size enough because your thighs will be so big the trousers won't get past them anyway.

So, no, I don't look like a cyclist. However, the more pertinent question for me is: 'Do I look like a writer?' Because, although some people don't understand it, I'm not paid to ride a bike, I'm paid to write.

Actually, I'm probably not a typical cycling journalist either. About half of the people I've met in the cycling media fell into it or got lucky having been keen riders first. The other half have more of a journalistic background. They're bike racing fans, and feel that elite cycle sport is a fascinating subject of study and a good route to professional respect. They're often correct. People like Jeremy Whittle, Matt Rendell, and my friends Chris Sidwells, Edward Pickering and Lionel Birnie are all rightly regarded as superb cycling historians and storytellers.

I'm somewhere down the middle. With dad having worked in a bicycle shop for 28 years, I've been around bikes all my life. Then I went to university and trained to be a professional journalist. But I'm not going to pretend

I've always been dedicated to a career in bike journalism (although it was somewhat foretold by my very first article, aged 11, for the school newspaper — a bike test of a Raleigh Streetwolf).

When I first went to university in Sheffield it was actually to study mechanical engineering. Twenty-one years ago when dad and I did our last French ride I had two heroes: Paul Stanley of the rock band Kiss and Damon Hill. I recognised rock stardom was a bit of a shot in the dark — although to this day I still harbour dreams — but becoming an F1 car designer seemed perfectly feasible. The problem was that I'd taken 'A' levels in English, Spanish, Art and General Studies. No worries, I figured, I'll just go to Sheffield Uni and do an engineering foundation year.

Unfortunately, I discovered two things in my first year in Sheffield. The first was that I really enjoyed dancing, drinking and rather hopefully putting myself in situations where brave or drunk young ladies might make the first move. The second thing I discovered was that I had absolutely no aptitude for pure maths or physics; two quite important chapters in an engineer's talent book.

What I did notice, though, was that I looked forward to every Monday morning after lectures where — like a junior Alan Partridge — I'd head home with a massive bottle of Sunny Delight and read Peter Hitchens in, back then, the *Daily Express*.

And here we go with some more of those stereotypes. 'What's a cyclist doing reading a conservative columnist like Peter Hitchens? Aren't we all lefty types?' Politically I have headed more to the left as I've grown older — which rather counters the old adage that people are socialists until they can afford not to be. But I still believe very much in self-determination, opportunity, and restricted interference from the state. In fact, I see those values being entirely in keeping with the freedom and self-empowerment that comes with cycling.

I still enjoy reading Peter Hitchens. And, he's a keen cyclist, too — so how's that for stereotype bashing? (A few years ago I pitched the idea to go for a ride with him as a feature article in a magazine I was writing for. My editor at the time, Luke Edwardes-Evans, gave it the green light, but I never worked up the nerve to try to contact Mr Hitchens. They say never meet your heroes. In this case, I decided not to even try.)

So I realised I'd always loved the news, and newspapers, and writing, and even broadcasting. With my engineering career already dead in the water, and with a great deal of luck and begging, I managed to wheedle my way into the University of Sheffield's vibrant journalism department where my course tutors were former *Observer* editor Donald Trelford and one of Fleet Street's finest reporters, Jonathan Foster. I spent three years learning shorthand, reporting from court, studying investigative work, and gaining my national journalism qualifications and degree. I also did shifts for the *Sun*'s 'Supergoals' website in Leeds, and worked as a radio reporter and newsreader during my holidays.

(Incidentally, one rule of journalism I took to heart is never to make yourself part of the story. So to see so many 'I's and 'my's in these pages is making me feel quite uncomfortable. But as this book is a memoir of sorts, I'll have to be forgiven.)

Looking back, it was really quite fun, but then with hindsight you tend to forget the bad bits. That's also something we're quickly discovering on this ride — God knows how we managed last time. We're a day in and it's already no laughing matter. My arse is really starting to feel the effects of that unbroken-in Brooks.

So far we haven't followed many of the same roads that we must have taken back in 1994, but our arrival in Vitré — a very pretty historic tourist trap with coachloads of elderly sightseers whose combined ages far outstrip that of the local landmarks — should solve all that and bring back memories.

It doesn't.

We stop at a boulangerie with an advert for the charmingly-named 'Roi Arthur' music festival in the window and buy three pains au chocolat and three pains aux raisins. Down the road — with me acting as the ride welfare officer — we buy seven half-litre bottles of water to fully refill our depleted reserves.

We stop for a drink, Matt passes over the suncream and I remove my gilet. There is a big range of cows here, black and white ones, some that are dark brown on top and others that are beige all over. There is no wind, it is overcast, but blue sky lies ahead with the threat of more hot weather. We had not really expected this sort of heat until south of the Loire.

On the upside, the unnerving shimmying that had set in on my bike yesterday has calmed down a bit today. I must say, I was not anticipating any problems at all with this bike. It is my pride and joy, which has spent most of its post-respray life in the spare bedroom. I have ridden it with four panniers before and it was trouble free. Perhaps it is much heavier this time?

I also noticed yesterday that my front wheel rubs against the brake blocks when I get out of the saddle. I didn't pay this much attention until we reached our campsite last night. It turned out that both our front wheel quick release levers had loosened somehow. I think somebody must have undone them, although Matt has mocked that idea. Fortunately, the QRs weren't loose enough for our front wheels to come out and for us to face-plant on the tarmac, but it's slightly worrying nonetheless.

These days all front forks have recesses so that even a completely loose quick release lever will not allow the front wheel to drop out. This has brought the number of fractured skulls down immensely. Running a bike shop, and before that a motorcycle dealership, not only made me paranoid about security but I also saw the after effects of poor maintenance or bad riding. Nobody looks pretty in hospital.

I've always really loved working. This is unquestionably due to my Victorian-style upbringing, mixed with a touch of the eremetic. An eremitic believes that the more miserable you are in this life, the greater your rewards will be in the next. This is something that many of my employers deeply believed in, and it is only now, with the benefit of hindsight, that I realise things can be different. In fact, it is only now that I realise that most people can barely do their job properly, and how they manage to keep in employment is puzzling. It must be the 'Peter Principle' — you get promoted to a position that you can just about manage — or usually not, but by then it is way too late to send you back to the ranks.

I certainly never had dreams of running a bike shop. As a lad, my dear late mother was very keen on me becoming an advocate: a fine, well-paid, profession and one that is at the very foundations of Jersey life. Sadly, I never got near my mother's wishes. Although nearly all my prep school chums had fathers who were in the legal profession, as I got older I tended to look for something a bit more exciting. And let us not forget, I am really a humble son of the soil. A few of my ancestors might have got lucky, but I am certain that dirty fingernails were involved somewhere along the way.

Similar to Matt, albeit more than 25 years earlier, my inclinations and teenage heroes pointed me towards the rasping bark of an open exhaust, or even the slick patter of a disc jockey reaching across the airwaves from a pirate radio station somewhere in the North Sea. The only interview I ever had with a careers advisor at the old alma mater did nothing to dampen my enthusiasm for these two rather ambitious careers, but it did little to further the cause, either.

Perhaps it was normal back then — remember, we're talking about the distant days of the late 1960s — to receive no advice on a career path. Living in Jersey, it appeared that if your parents did not want to pay for you to follow an engineering course at some far-flung university then you had to get some brilliant 'A' level results. If you did, then all the car manufacturers, even Rolls-Royce, would be fighting to employ you. Possibly even throwing large sums of money in your direction.

My father subscribed to this view as well: if you really want to become an engineering apprentice then the job fairy will visit you and turn you into a genius. Unfortunately, the job fairy must have been busy that year because no matter how hard I tried, I never reached the academic heights that my fellow 'A' level physics, chemistry and maths buddies got to. Although I had done well at secondary school initially, my academic life took something of a dive after my mum died when I was 13. It's funny how much of your life is shaped by what happens before the ages of 16 or 18 — arguably the time when you're least able to make the correct choices or react wisely to events.

In my youth, not only did you have to follow a regime established on the pages of Tom Brown's School Days, but the range of subjects you could study was severely limited. You had to follow either all science subjects or all arts subjects, with no crossover whatsoever. This proved to be rather wasteful because I was very good at art but I was forced to abandon it. Even my father, in an unfamiliar moment of sound career advice, said that the architect's life was the life for me as I was so handy with the crayons.

Sadly, with mum gone I was very much in dad's hands and his perceptions weren't quite so clear when he and my brother suggested I follow a career in the Royal Navy as a helicopter pilot. I can hardly see anything without a strong pair of glasses. However, it took all my effort not only to make dad understand the serious impediment this might be to any airborne-come-seabound career, but also to convince the Navy careers officer when he phoned up.

Ideas for my future came thick and fast from various people, none of whom it could be said were massively successful on the career front. One of the most interesting — or, indeed, one of the most alarming — also came from my father, who suggested that I join the Jesuit priesthood, an organisation which at that time had a seminary in Jersey. His thinking was that the food was exceptional and you'd get an unsurpassed grounding in the law thrown in for good measure.

I am no genius, but I am fairly certain I would have regretted abandoning my teenage freedom — and who knows what else — just for some free training in the law. So my last year in education was scholastically appalling, but very good socially. I hated every moment at school, due without doubt to my frustration in the classroom. After a year struggling to achieve any kind of academic success to underwrite my future in the motor industry, I very happily left school without even the germ of an idea of what to do next. Which is quite often the standard preparation for a career in the bike trade.

At first I had a job at the local tomato box factory. In the season we worked every day, apart from Sunday when we only did mornings. There were two main benefits to this job: firstly it paid well; and secondly, because *you were so tired when you finished, you went straight to bed and never spent any money.*

That said, around this time I did manage to muster just enough energy to work as a disc jockey in the evenings. I didn't have my own car back then and it was difficult to get about without one. I used to load up my records in two sports bags and walk five miles into Saint Helier, do the gig, and hope that I'd be paid there and then. If so, I could afford to get a taxi home and maybe buy some chips.

I only started working in a bike shop in June 1981 when I was 29. At the time, I was running a motorbike shop but my boss had opened a new store. Motorcycle sales began shrinking and bicycles started becoming more popular. It's nothing to be proud of, but I've done the equivalent of two life sentences (with good behaviour) in the bike trade. It's good honest toil but, like being a paperboy, there are overtones of the enthusiastic teenager about it. So be careful if you're hoping for a career.

Dad and I follow good roads out of Vitré and we make decent progress, but it's hardly fun. Who thought up this route? Meanwhile, we continue to struggle to remember any of it. Thankfully traffic is fairly light. All we see are some municipal vehicles: run-down old bangers that no self-respecting council employee in Britain would be seen dead driving. In fact, they probably wouldn't be classed as drivable under EU health and safety laws — laws which the relatively europhobic Brits seem to follow to the letter, but which our europhile Continental cousins are often content to ignore.

At a pleasant bridge over the river in a village called Gennes we stop so dad can take one of his painkillers. It is rather a performance as he breaks the pill into little pieces and then uses a tidal wave of water from his unlidded bottle to wash it all down, effing and blinding in the process. The more time you spend with him, the more you remember what an odd fella the old fella is. How does anybody reach the age of 63 and not learn how to swallow a pill? Still, at least we can all rest easy that he won't develop an addiction to prescription painkillers.

The whole scene isn't improved much by the fact dad has separated his money into various hard-to-steal places, one of which is a wallet that hangs round his neck under his clothes and pokes forward beneath his T-shirt similar to Darth Vader's iron lung. This pill-taking scene is like being with some kind of unoiled robot having a seizure.

As we hop back on our bikes I realise we are both mounting them from the left, our bodies exposed to passing traffic. I wonder if that's because it's somehow easier to swing your right leg over? Or is it because we ride on the left at home so it's the safest way to get on board from a British pavement? Do the French mount their bikes from the right? I resolve to keep my eye out, although for all the talk about France being such a cycling country, we've seen precious few bike riders.

Matt and I stop at Gennes sur Seiche for a bite to eat and I remember to swallow the anti-inflammatory pills that I have been prescribed to combat the plantar faciistis (heel pain) that I have. Cycling is good for this particular ailment, though, so it's feeling a lot better. I'm a big wuss when it comes to taking medication, so as well as breaking the pills in two I also chew them. Then, to ensure a generous gush of water to speed them on their way, I remove the top from my drinking bottle and take a hearty swig. I wonder if a greater number of smaller pills could be the answer for me?

Of course, 'smaller' in any sense isn't seen as manly. When I first started selling bikes there was a move for the macho man to always ask for a 25in 'full size' frame. It was an eye opener, and not only for me, especially as most people were way too short to ever contemplate a frame half that size. Time moves on and these days it is hard to find a 25in frame, even if your masculinity demands it.

Then there were the people who would come in the day before a big organised charity ride, who wanted all the gear (with very little idea) and demanded instant attention because they were doing what they called "The Race" tomorrow. How sad is that? Surely it is noble enough to raise money for charity without bigging yourself up by saying you're going "racing". They normally looked like they sat behind a desk eating pies, never mind being ready to compete on a bicycle.

I'll never forget the guy who asked me for some "disraeli gears" for his bike. Disraeli Gears *happened to be one of my favourite 'long playing' albums (I think they're called 'vinyls' now) and I have a rare stereo copy. But I sold him some derailleur gears instead. He seemed just as happy.*

Probably my all time favourite memory from the bike trade is the 'one finger lift'. This is when some sage person, taking great care to find the point of balance on the top tube, picks a bike up using only his index finger. If they can do that with consummate ease, then it's the true benchmark of a quality bicycle (I'm being sarcastic here, by the way). In the iconic scenario, you get a group of these connoisseurs all vying to do the old one finger lift with much nodding and murmuring of appreciation. If only weight was the one thing that defined a good bike. The lightest bike I ever had was as flexible as a 12in ruler and some of my best efforts simply went in bending the frame, not driving me forward.

And here's one last story for people who think I'm paranoid about security. One day in the run-up to Christmas a woman came in to collect a bike, but it appeared that the bike was not there. We remembered taking the money, as the customer had bought it on the 'Christmas Club', so wondered if somebody had been given the wrong bike by mistake. A few days passed while we tried hard to work out the best solution to the problem. The denouement came the following Monday, when the woman's husband called the shop. It appeared that 'Mr Smith' had been married twice. His current wife had purchased the bike for one of the children from the first marriage, but she had had to go into hospital for a minor operation. While she was being treated, wife number one had assumed her identity and, armed with the child and the description of the bike, went and collected the bike from our shop without telling her ex. Beautiful, huh?

Matt and I ride on and pass through Craon during the two hours-come-seven-days that France seems to be shut for lunch. The streets are deserted. This allows me to take a good selection of photos without having any bystanders creeping into shot, although I had expected most Craons to be quite colourful. (That's a little joke).

For aesthetic reasons, dad decides to remove the drying washing that is hanging from the back of his bike before taking his photos at Craon. I leave mine as it is. A large part of the reason for doing this ride is because I thought it would make for a good story. But I've also learned that, like speaking to your mother, the best way to approach journalism is with complete honesty.

I've been a cycling journalist for 12 years. After graduating, Manda and I moved to London. Manda had studied in Brighton while I was in Sheffield, so it was a relief to finally live as a couple. But although Manda could easily find a teaching position, media and journalism hopefuls aren't exactly in short supply in the capital. I ended up cleaning vans and hire cars in Kingston-upon-Thames for a year to make ends meet while also applying for journalism jobs. There were moments of interest, such as delivering vehicles to the McLaren F1 team and the set of a James Bond movie, and my boss from back then is still one of my dearest friends. But I think it's fair to say I was growing increasingly bitter as I faced rejection after rejection.

After a year I decided to give up the vans and spend all my time just applying for the jobs I wanted. Somehow I found myself being commissioned to write a book — *100 Strangest Unexplained Mysteries* (not a Pulitzer Prize winner, although there is a girl in Nova Scotia who ranks it above Harry Potter in her homepage's list of favourite things). Then I finally got lucky with a 'proper' job. I started with IPC Media's cycling department on April 28, 2003 and spent five years as a sub-editor working on *Cycling Weekly*, *Cycle Sport* and *Mountain Bike Rider*. Subs are essentially the bottom wipers, face savers and turd polishers. They have to make sure a writer's words are all correct, make sense and they won't get the mag or paper sued. Any reporter who doesn't buy his subs chocolates at Christmas is really not doing himself any favours.

After a couple of years I also started doing a few writing jobs — mainly feature stories about professional bike racing. I've ridden alongside Bernard Hinault; accosted a sweaty Robbie Hunter outside a Milton Keynes hotel; enjoyed a conference call with Jan Ullrich and a German translator; ambled along the Thames cyclepath with Mr and Mrs Chris Hoy; and even played darts with Geraint Thomas on the eve of a Tour de France prologue. I've been a regular contributor to *Cycling Weekly*, interviewer for *Guitar and Bass Magazine*, then for the first five years after it launched I was chief writer for *Cycling Active*.

Throughout it all, the one principle I have tried to follow in my professional life invokes the words of Jean-Jacques Rousseau's: "If I am not better, at least I am different."

In many ways cycle journalism and the cycle trade, just as any other sector, lives in its own little bubble. So early on I decided I wanted to try to link the bike with normal people's every day lives. I wanted to show that cycling doesn't have to be your whole life, but it can be a really beautiful addendum to it. It is something that gets you fit almost by proxy on the invigorating commute to work. It is something that lets you relax and momentarily forget the daily worries that come with modern life. It is something that can help you connect in a strangely special way with family and friends on a shared ride.

This voyage across France, I hope, is a testament to that last element.

As we leave Craon I pop into a Système-U supermarket and pick up some water, oranges, dried apricots and bananas. Dad chats to an old lady outside the shop. Like most of the women we've come across, she is an ideal candidate for the French female pensioner tug of war team and has teeth like Stonehenge (after Clark Griswold has reversed into it).

We get back on track. And in a repeat of yesterday we find ourselves rolling along another long, straight road, now with a headwind and the sun beating down. Tonight I'm going to study the maps a lot harder and reroute us away from this set of instructions. Eventually I have to stop. Sweat is getting into my eyes, effectively blinding me, so dad lends me his Buff to use as a headband.

As well as the sun we've also been followed by an agricultural smell for a lot of the day. It can't be the old chap because he's been behind me, and even he can't project farts forward. In any case, the cause has been quite obvious: huge, steaming piles of manure in roadside fields welcoming us to this part of the world. Funnily enough, it is only with a few miles to go that dad comments on it. His sense of smell and taste is all but extinct — we suspect from his time working as a silkscreen printer — and the whiff that finally gets through is far from the most offensive we've had today. But I wonder if his loss of taste is the reason he doesn't seem particularly fussed about eating these days.

Despite the 'mal odour', this particular road at least has quite a pleasant destination. After a gentle descent we find ourselves in a churchyard overlooking the picturesque valley town of Segré, its bridges spanning the L'Oudon river below. We even manage to buy a sandwich from a town centre boulangerie — praise be — although attempts to procure further non-bread-based supplies from the Spa general store over the road prove to be both literally and metaphorically fruitless. Apparently the bloke who runs the shop is on holiday. Ha ha ha. This country.

We climb out of Segré, relatively happy in the knowledge that our goal for the day, Vern d'Anjou is within touching distance.

We stop for photos at Saint Quentin les Anges, where there is an almost life-size display of characters from Asterix the Gaul made from papier maché. Then it's on to our destination. Vern d'Anjou is quiet but we manage to find the camping just behind the village's leisure centre. There is no one here, not even any other campers. A notice board informs us that there is only an on-site welcome between 09.00hrs to 12.00hrs, and then between 14.00hrs to 17.00hrs. We arrived at 17.01. It also says unauthorised camping is punishable by summary execution, or something similar. Matt says in no uncertain terms that whatever happens, we'll take our chances here.

Thankfully it never comes to that. I follow the instructions on the board and ring a number. As I speak into the phone, a chap in overalls arrives in a white van. Immediately he says he has forgotten something, so he departs with some haste but reappears minutes later. I hope that he has not forgotten the keys to 'les sanitaires'. He has no change, but as the cost is almost six euros, I give him the full six and don't worry about it.

He provides me with a detailed site visit, explaining all the facilities thoroughly, especially the visitors' book. With only five pitches and no one else in sight, I have to admire his optimism. He leaves us to our own devices and I imagine he returns to his regular day job.

Seemingly there's nobody else here at Vern d'Anjou's pretty sorry-looking campsite, although 'Monsieur Overalls' who speaks to dad assures us a clapped-out caravan down the end is inhabited (I have my doubts) and a campervan is due to arrive tonight. We have the pick of the pitches and camp up next to the shower block. We also have the code to get in the impressively clean and tidy facilities — I won't give it away to protect the site's limited income, but it involves a date that can't go down well with German visitors.

I shower and tend to those regions that really shouldn't be discussed by Englishmen. The new Brooks saddle is taking its toll. I thoroughly wash, dry and then (perhaps unwisely) follow the old chap's advice of scrubbing the affected parts — which have begun to bleed — with a wet wipe. Then I apply calendular cream. Quite frankly I have never felt pain like it. My perineum — that's the bit between your bottom and your 'not-bottom' — is on fire.

We put up the tent and do the chores. Matt is in some pain and goes for a shower. I also have a shock in the toilets when I realise my urine is coffee coloured. Thank goodness I am aware of the dehydration problems that cycling brings on and manage not to faint. Back in 1994 I went a day or two without even peeing at all, so drinking gallons of water was a high priority from the start this time. Obviously more drink is required, and I make a mental note to up my intake.

Our pitch is just beside the main route to the swimming baths, so dinner is frequently interrupted by very polite teenagers who 'bonjour' their way to the piscine. Thankfully they stop 'bonjouring' by the time I want to go to sleep.

A little later, after I've recovered from my painful shower episode, dad and I lie on the grass for dinner, which is pretty limited: a ham and cheese baguette from Segré, oranges, bananas and water. It's hardly food for kings of the road. Afterwards I decide to have a potter round the wider — I use the term advisedly — site. There's a little children's play centre, the back of a primary school, a football pitch, a small field with goats, the leisure centre, and a sweet little lido where a swimming club is having its Monday night training sessions.

One thing I started doing yesterday was to take photos of anything that said 'David', 'Davey', 'Dave', 'Ad', 'Addy' or 'Adam' to send back to the boys. I've seen loads of 'Ads' but not many for David, however a defibrillator by the pool is emblazoned with 'AED / DAE' so I email that home — it's close enough.

With my exploring instincts sated and the sun well set, I get in the tent and look over the maps for tomorrow. Dad's already primed for bed. I finally switch my torch off at about 10pm only to find more church bells ringing out yonder. This time they repeat the hour peal two minutes after the hour, and they do a solitary ring on the quarter hour. Doesn't God have some sort of style guide for his franchises?

Thought for the day: Dad tells me he takes his showers with his sandals on. Which is unusual.

RIDES OF PASSAGE

DAY 3
Health
Matters

Tuesday August 16, 1994 — Saint Julien to Argenton les Vallées (70 miles)
Tuesday August 4, 2015 — Vern d'Anjou to Argenton les Vallées (57.2 miles)

Matt aged 15

After a terrible night's sleep due to a bad sleeping mat, cats outside our tent and a church bell that started ringing at 3am, we got up at 6.30am. We packed all our stuff and, to our surprise - not! - saw Graham.

Once we knew Graham was awake we left as soon as possible. We quickly covered the 14km we were down from yesterday to Candé. Here we bought some waffles and three bottles of water. Not stopping for long, we set off for Louraix, at the top of an extremely steep hill that had the names of Tour de France winners on the tarmac.

We had a short break but set off again, aiming for Bécon. We arrived here quickly and Dad bought a phone card to ring Mum. We tried it in a phone booth but Mum must have been out. Further on, at Saint Georges we lost a load of time but Dad at least managed to get a battery for the camera.

From Saint Georges we headed downhill to Chalonnes, which meant we would have to cross the Loire. Dad took some pictures but we didn't stay long. Coming out of Chalonnes meant we had to climb right out of the Val de Loire. We took quite a while to get to La Jumellière, where Dad bought some water and ice-creams. Here we also spoke to a French lady. Dad meant to ask her to put our rubbish in her bin, but actually asked her to put the rubbish on her lawn!

On the way to Chemillé I almost got run-over by an HGV as I was not concentrating and missed a stop line. In Chemillé, Dad tried to ring Mum but to no avail, and I had to put some Tiger Balm on my back. We stayed here for ages and then left for Vihiers. In Vihiers we bought a baguette, some saucisson, some chocolates, two hats, some peaches, nectarines and two bottles of cider.

We got slightly lost coming out of Vihiers but eventually took the right road to Argenton. This road lasted 20km and was murder. We entered Argenton by a steep descent and had to climb up to the campsite.

The guy in charge was not about, so Dad went to find him and I fell asleep with the bikes. Dad woke me and had brought a cold ice tea - it tasted great. We put the tent up eventually and I went for a shower. We ate dinner, bread, saucisson and the remainder of the cheese, then went to phone Mum. After trying loads of times we got through and had a chat. I put some calendular cream on my sore bits. I feel really bad. Dad managed to find another boring little friend at the campsite.

We went to sleep at 10.30pm-ish. We travelled 110.7km today.

Arthur aged 42

Our new friend Graham saw us off — bless his heart. Got a good start today, but as France is open for business the roads are quite busy. As usual, the first few kilometres flew by, perhaps inspired by the multi-colour inscriptions on the road: 'Jacky Durand', obviously a local hero who rode this year's Tour de France. Further on, the ascent into Le Louroux had 'Rominger' painted on the road. What a shame that our camera had a flat battery.

Plenty of water and stops for Matt. Managed to get a camera battery at Saint Georges, and we busily snapped away at anything in case the film was damaged by opening the camera.

Crossed the Loire over a series of bridges into Chalonnes. Very much a tourist haven. Would have liked to have stopped, but the streets were choc-a-bloc.

Matt grovelling a bit after lunch but better than yesterday. Bought more water at La Jumillière and two Cornetto-type things. Gave our old bottles to a kind lady, who I advised to put them in the lawn instead of in the rubbish. I said 'pelouse' instead of 'poubelle'.

Bought a phone card at Bécon Le Granite. No one at home when I phoned. Bought provisions at Vihiers: saucisson; baguette; peaches; nectarines and a bottle of cider. Finally made Argenton after quite a struggle. Walked up the hill to the best campsite yet.

Dined and managed to get through to home after six or seven attempts. Ate up my 40 franc phone card, still well worth it. Highlights of the day:

— The campsite is good.

— Matt fell asleep on the grass verge while I went to pay for our pitch.

— Unfortunately the taps and showers are cold.

— Good dinner again: saucisson, Bon Bel and cider.

Matt aged 36

It's 6.45am, my arse is still on fire and I've woken up. Actually, I say 'woken up', it's more like I've simply decided to stop closing my eyes. I had a terrible night, more bells ringing and there was a storm at some point. I'm really not sleeping well. Dad says he thought another set of campers arriving at some point in the night and he has heard people going into the showers. So although he's been awake for a while, he hasn't gone for a wash — he's waiting for them to come out. I'm not convinced and get up and go to investigate. Nope, nobody around. (Incidentally, for the whole time we've been here, we've seen nobody enter or leave the caravan down the end. I think it's a phoney 'van, just there to make it look like somebody's using the site.)

However, there is one little surprise in the shower block. I go to do my teeth and notice that there's now a warning sign cable-tied to the same tap I used to wash my face and brush my teeth last night. 'Robinet Legionel' it says. My French is just about passable. I know 'robinet' means 'tap', so I can only assume 'Legionel' means it contains Legionnaires' disease. I issue forth a profanity. That tag wasn't there last night — I wasn't so tired that I would have ignored a sign threatening Legionnaires' disease — I can only assume that the sounds dad heard this morning was 'Monsieur Overalls' returning to do a little job that must have slipped his mind yesterday. If the French spent as much time on health and safety as they do building churches this would be a far better country. Having said that, nobody seems to do any work anyway — perhaps they're all trying to get some sleep in between the bloody bell rings.

My heart rate-testing behaviour yesterday probably reveals that I am something of a hypochondriac. In fact, that was part of the inspiration behind doing this trip. I thought that if I could cycle 1,000 kilometres across France I would have to reason with myself that I am actually in decent physical shape. I'm not joking: every twinge in the chest is an early heart attack; every lump in my body is a cancerous growth. I've currently got a slightly blurry eye that comes and goes, and which I'm still considering might be the effect of some form of brain tumour. So, right now, believing I may have ingested a possibly fatal bacteria has left me a trifle concerned.

But I have other pressing duties. I apply calendular cream again to my backside and a repeat of the fiery balls episode of yesterday. Then we go through the routine of packing everything away.

When the old chap is otherwise engaged, I Google 'Legionnaires' disease'. I've started to feel a little strange just thinking about it, although my preliminary investigations say symptoms take between two and 12 days to surface. Oh man, what if we get almost to the end of this ride, then I realise I've caught this? Shall we just go home now? I really am in a mild panic.

Arthur aged 63

Up early at 07.00hrs again. The idea is that the early mornings are much cooler and we can cover a good mileage before the heat slows us down. The best-laid plans, of course, occasionally go awry.

No one arrived during the night so this could be the most exclusive campsite in the whole of France. Or the least-known campsite. Or perhaps the initial formalities and the wait for the guardian to appear might be putting people off.

Still, it's not our problem. Matt is not feeling too good, particularly around one delicate area. This is the result of fitting a brand-new Brooks leather saddle without doing the obligatory 500 miles or more running-in period. Furthermore, he has discovered that the tap he used last night to clean his teeth now has a label that suggests that it might be contaminated with Legionnaires' disease (French Foreign Legionnaires' disease I imagine?). This naturally sends him into a state of some concern, although he seems more vexed that the label has mysteriously become attached during the night, rather than any implications of impending ill health. Fortunately I know that Matt is a hypochondriac so I do not worry too much, and it did take his mind off his other problem.

For some reason, when we were getting our bikes ready back in Jersey dad fitted his water bottle cages so the one that is easiest to reach holds the huge 1.5-litre bottle — which you have to stop riding to remove and quaff from — while his normal-size water bottle is sitting less conveniently on the seat tube. I find this very odd, as I think it's important to continually reach down and swig from my normal cycling bottle all the time, using the big bottle as a reservoir to refill from at stops. Dad just doesn't seem very keen on drinking on the go and he is paranoid about growing germs of some kind in his water bottle. He suggests he might throw his cycling bottle away because he hasn't washed it for two days (although it was brand new when we started). He asks if I want to throw mine away too?

I point out that I may have just ingested water containing Legionella bacteria, so, all things considered, I'll take my chance with a two-day old water bottle, thank you very much. I also say, if he can just wait a bit longer we'll buy something to wash the bottles with.

"Ah yes, Milton tablets should do the trick," he replies. Considering we've only seen about three shops open in more than 100 miles, I think that might be a bit hopeful.

"Well, you might have to do with Fairy Liquid," I reply, slightly irritated.

I still can't work out if his fussing is a sign of age or if he's always been like this. I remember when Ad and Davey were two or three he refused to eat some of their birthday cake because they had rather too enthusiastically blown out the candles with a fine spray of spittle. Thinking about it, I'm pretty sure he's always been like this.

With a few things on my mind, I again make the old British cyclists' faux pas and head out of the campsite on the wrong side of its access road. I hate being both narked and stupid.

It's too much to hope for that we might get some interesting, varied roads to take my mind off things, but at least dad is on the case for food this morning. After our first long straight session to the village of La Pouëze he pops into a little shop. I stay outside to guard the bikes, text Manda and mum to tell them of my impending doom, and go online with my phone to find out more about Legionnaires' disease. Apparently symptoms include muscle ache, tiredness, high temperatures and confusion. If either dad or I get it, how will we ever know?

I'm distracted at one point by a car that goes past and its exhaust falls off right in front of me. Then I spot a woman in her dressing gown, walking her dog. In my eyes, this country is not doing itself any favours.

At least my bit of web surfing has averted the Legionella disaster. The NHS website — ah, good old British NHS — says the disease mainly gets old folk and children, and it seems you have to breathe it in. So what about the shower at the campsite last night, then? Best not to think about it.

Matt stays outside while I go into the shop at Pouëze and try as hard as I can to buy lots of food and some washing up liquid to clean our drinking bottles. Matt has told me that he needs plenty of fuel to cycle well, which may go some way to explaining why he has a 38-inch waist and I have a 32-inch waist. But, in fairness, he has not reached the 'manopause' yet and consequently has not been overcome with the blatant vanity that I exhibit.

It is a very big shop and it could accommodate a lot more stuff inside. Between the modern-looking shelves is enough room to drive a Mini and most of my time is lost walking around looking for things. I'm impressed by the technology that this shop has, especially as nothing in the area suggests that anything else has changed since the War years. The assistant scans my purchases with a barcode reader and giggles in appreciation when I say how modern her shop is. She tells me that she thinks there are more cars on the road nowadays, which certainly seems absolutely correct to us, even if some of the cars arguably shouldn't be on the roads in the first place.

By now we have biscuits, cakes, oranges and a banana in our larder, so we are probably OK for the next mile or two.

Dad emerges from the shop with — incredibly — a bottle of the French equivalent of Fairy Liquid. I'm starting to think that the old fella can command anything he wants, he just doesn't want the same things I do.

I'm still not very switched on, and after feasting on biscuits I foolishly leave my helmet perched atop a dustbin as we set off. I am truly a gumby this morning. About 300 yards down the road dad spots I'm not wearing it and goes back at full speed to pick it up. Certainly there's no questioning the old fella's fitness. Despite his bad heel, and no sense of smell or taste, he's in impressive shape for a man aged 63.

I spent an hour last night with the real Michelin road map and the Google Maps app on my phone, but I really can't do much about this initial part of today's route. We're heading towards Saint George and then over the Loire to Chalonnes, crossing the exact same bridges we used last time. For the occasion, in my handlebar bag I even have a retro T-shirt I wore back in 1994.

Sure enough we sort of recognise Saint George, or at least the Marie — which is an impressive structure — and try to recreate a photograph from back in the day. Then we do the same on the bridge over the Loire. It's very scenic. The river is quite low but the sky is beautifully blue. It's about 11.30am and the sun is just starting to warm up. Some days back home I would only just about be warming up myself by 11.30, too, but we've already done 20 miles this morning.

We recognise Chalonnes and dad takes some pictures while a band plays along the river bank. There's a lot of activity here today: it's easily the most bustling town we've been to so far and we have to climb carefully up the main street while people dive off the pavements.

We are on a similar route to last time because the villages that we pass through sound familiar, and probably look familiar too, but they all have the same format which generally includes a rather magnificent church. One has to wonder how these places keep going, as they are out of proportion to the rest of the village. I wonder about this for a while and arrive at the conclusion that there is terrible carnage on the roads on a daily basis, and the resulting funerals keep these churches in business. Another thing that catches my imagination is the abundance of crosses at the roadside — I think that these are called 'cavalries' — I wonder if these were a religious version of the roadside bouquet that has become so fashionable these days?

We want to retrace our steps as closely as we can today in an effort to replicate some of the photos that we took on the last occasion we were here. We succeed and are able to revisit the Loire bridge crossing picture. During our photo stop we are passed by two mountain bikers who look exactly like mountain bikers everywhere, with small rucksacks on their backs and baggy shorts. However, they do show some originality: they have their socks hanging off their handlebar ends, drying in the breeze.

A short distance further on we cross the Loire again on a much grander bridge, which leads us into Chalonnes sur Loire. I take more photos, again virtually in the same place as 21 years ago, and chat to a Frenchman who is towing a single-wheel trailer behind him. He is on a short tour from his home in Brittany, so although he looks equipped to cross Continents, he has not actually cycled that far.

We stop at another artisan boulangerie 'Festival des Pains' at Chalonnes. It seems rather a pity that something as uniquely French as a baker's shop — which like churches are a 'must have' in every village — appears to have become a chain of almost identical establishments. Our ham baguettes taste great, as do the soft drinks that we wash them down with.

Life isn't entirely rosy, though. One rather unfortunate incident happens outside the boulangerie as an extremely elderly lady wishes me: "Merde à cyclistes" ("Shit to cyclists"). I feel that this is a rather unnecessary comment, given I am minding my own business. I manage to refrain from asking her if she spent the war years on her back, or how long did she have before she was due to depart this life. Instead I keep quiet and hopefully take the moral high ground.

I must remember that I'm no spring chicken either these days, although my mortality isn't something that unduly worries me. They say you can't buy your health, but you can ruin it. Somehow I didn't manage to ruin mine — I do not know how exactly, because I certainly gave it a good go.

I started smoking when I was 13, only finally giving up when I started doing motorcycle trials and Matt was born in my mid-20s. My lack of stamina had no bearing on how good I was at motorcycle trials, but it did raise its head when I had to pick my motorbike up out of the mud, which was very often because I was rubbish. I was very keen on motorbikes as a teenager and came within a whisker of having my dad buy me a pukka Greeves 'Scottish' trials motorbike. Alas, when my older brother Bernard inspected it, he discovered it had a cracked crankcase that was difficult to mend. So bye-bye to that idea, but hello to the £5 that dad saved.

As a child I continued riding up and down banks on my pushbike, which isn't quite the same thing as trials riding, but this too stopped when I broke the handlebar stem. Consequently, I never had that early age training so necessary to achieving anything in sport these days. When I did eventually buy a motorbike to do trials, far too much alcohol had passed through me to ever hope of rediscovering the balance of my youth.

Supporting the brewing industry seemed like the most natural thing in the world back then. Everyone went to the pub and it was a little world in itself. Also, unlike home with my dad, it was a world that was welcoming, friendly and had food available at all times. The public bar of the Royal Hotel in Saint Martin in Jersey was like home and at least there were people there. Maybe slightly seedy people whose through-put of fags and alcohol stayed at a remarkably constant level while the place was open, but very welcoming nonetheless.

You certainly saw life in all its glory there. One event that I still recall clearly was during an early evening, when a gentleman propping up the bar gave in to his natural inclinations and managed to overflow his (admittedly short) Wellingtons. I've never seen that happen again.

If I had ever developed a drink problem, I would be able to pinpoint the cause quite easily. As a child there was very rarely any medicine in the house. I remember most of my common ailments being treated by that traditional remedy: strong drink. Fortunately, I was generally in good health, but should I have had a cold or sore throat, it required the application of a half-pint glass of hot water, sugar and whatever spirit was around. This was normally either rum or cognac. I did not particularly like the flavour, but after half a glass I was beyond caring, and I slept well.

My only serious bout of illness occurred when I was three or four and I had an abscess in my ear. I am only guessing that it must have been a worry, because even now I remember the outpouring of kindness from all and sundry. During this period lots of unusual things happened: I was supplied with an endless assortment of lemonades; my dad went to a toy shop and bought two cast model racing cars; and the woman who lived up the lane brought over one of those gigantic Christmas crackers that are full of charms and trinkets. All for me! I think I also had real medicine, in the shape of penicillin tablets that were crushed up and fed to me in a spoonful of jam. Perhaps I should try that method these days rather than my current technique with those painkillers.

I remember that penicillin was a popular remedy for most ailments back in the '50s. Our family doctor spent much of his visit looking down my throat, using an enormous spoon that my mum supplied. The doctor's name was O'Connor, but as a three-year-old, I knew him as 'Doctor Old Connor'. To be fair, my hearing was probably not that good at the time.

In my wilderness years after leaving school, as I roamed from pub to pub, I quite often fell ill due to the poor hygiene found in these places. My dad's preferred cure for diarrhea was a generous glass of the French anise-based liqueur, Ricard. The only other complaint that dogged me in those days, *apart from raging hangovers, was the common cold. My cure for a cold was, unsurprisingly, also alcohol-based. Never mind all the concoctions on the chemist's shelf, my salvation rested in a quarter bottle of 'Captain Morgan' rum. This was initially taken in the time-honoured fashion with sugar and hot water, but usually ended up being drunk neat from the bottle.*

I suspect that this may have lacked any medicinal foundation as a cure but it worked well by taking away the symptoms for a few hours, and the following day you had such a bad hangover that a cold was the least of your worries.

So I imagine that the good health I enjoy at present is probably down to my genes, rather than a very self-controlled lifestyle. And thanks, too, to my wife who takes great care of me, even if I don't always take her advice.

We stop for lunch by Chalonnes's town square, where there is a market in full flow. Dad emerges from the boulangerie with a sandwich, some water, and a can of iced tea. I've decided I'm going to keep an emergency can of soft drink in one of my panniers, just in case. I try to find some shade behind a bus shelter while we eat our sandwich, but I can't really sit down and my off-the-bike movements are rather hampered by perineal injuries.

I'm reminded of the old joke from *Carry On... Again Doctor* when Jim Dale and Peter Gilmore are young medics guessing passing patients' ailments. Peter Butterworth comes shuffling past, very slowly, looking pained, so they make their guesses before both going up to him. Jim Dale says: "Excuse me sir but my friend and I, we're doing spot diagnosis and I was wondering if you could help me. Now I'd say you've got haemorrhoids and he thinks it's a slipped disc. Could you tell us?"

Peter Butterworth replies: "Let me see now. You thought it was a slipped disc? I'm afraid you were wrong. And you thought it was haemorrhoids? I'm afraid you were wrong. As a matter of fact, I thought I was going to break wind... I'm afraid I was wrong." (Just for the record, I only have sore bits. I haven't soiled myself, although the effect is the same.)

I know from studying the map last night that our official route out of Chalonnes is uphill and involves another pesky 'D' road. It also doesn't seem to go in a particularly straight line, heading due south before veering eastwards to our goal for the day at Argenton. So I've prepared an alternative route, which we pick up a couple of miles out of Chalonnes. We turn left, cross the other lane of the big road, and head under a rail bridge onto a real country lane.

It's so like the kinds of roads I'm used to riding back home that I lapse into riding on the left momentarily again. But this is more like it. It's a route that gently meanders, with no central line down the middle, and trees, bushes and nature are all within touching distance, not on the other side of vast expanses. So far our journey has felt very much like watching a movie while on rollers or a turbo-trainer — we've seen France pass by each side while we've sweated, ploughing on almost mindlessly ahead. Now we're starting to feel really in among the landscape.

The problem, here, though, is that it's much easier to get lost. I take the wrong turn and send us up a hill so steep — way above 10 per cent gradient — that we really can do no more than get off and push. Then I have to get the phone out and use Google Maps to see exactly where we are. It's not a big problem to get back on course and we would have had to climb at some point. But I realise if we are going to go freestyle with our route I'll have to use my phone more, which will require data roaming, which is really going to kill my battery power. Hey-ho. Let's just get where we're going for now.

At the top of the hill we're in farmland, following narrow but smooth lanes between fields. There's so much more to see, the threat of long-distance humpbacks is gone, and for the first time on this trip dad and I get the chance to chat properly. We make good time. In fact, it's almost like doing a sportive back home in England. Despite my physical pain in the saddle, we're pretty happy and even the sun isn't going crazy today — it's warm, but not mentally hot.

'Mentally hot'. Now that's an interesting term. I mentioned earlier about my hypochondria, which is hilarious in certain circumstances but not in the midst of an episode, but I also suffer from something else: anxiety attacks. I have had a very happy life, if I was religious and egotistical enough I'd even say I'd been blessed. But anxiety and panic has been the one thing over the last 13 years to blight it.

I can remember exactly when they started. It was in my last year in Sheffield and we were having a lecture by a chap from the Football Association. I remember feeling something very strange. It wasn't just a desire to get out of the room, it was an almost unstoppable urge to leave. I felt like I was losing all control over my actions, that I would shout out or scream something. I was getting hot, twitchy, and I slunk lower and lower in my seat gripping the edge of the table as if it was my last hold on reality.

I know it doesn't sound like much. So you get hot and sweaty and a bit worried? Big deal. But a panic attack induces a kind of mind-scrambling terror quite unlike anything else. In that first instance, and every instance ever since, I managed to stick it out until the situation I was in finished.

People don't like talking about mental illness. Considering a lot of folk seem perfectly happy to even go on telly with their manky or misshapen private parts, mental health is probably the last great health taboo. And what has affected me is really only low-level stuff — it's effectively mental conditioning that's gone wrong. But I think it's important to talk about it, because nobody would be ashamed if they had a broken arm, so why be ashamed if your brain wiring has gone a bit off-kilter. Also, let's be honest, how many people do you know who you would say are completely psychologically sound? I always say the difference between me and anybody else is that I recognise I have a problem.

I'm convinced my panic attacks were at least partly caused by chemicals. At this point, a lot of people would talk about marijuana or ecstasy or cocaine. However, I've never taken any illegal drugs. Never. In my youth I liked girls, rock 'n' roll, and alcohol, in that order. But by the time I was in my last year at uni I was with Manda (who was 200 miles away in Brighton) so in the evenings I ended up in the pub quite a lot. I think I probably overdid it. On the first occasion a panic attack hit, I'd been out the night before and the mixture of hangover and probably some underlying worry that in a few months the real world was waiting for me, acted as the catalyst for a fierce episode of acute anxiety.

The problem is, once you have one panic attack, you end up conditioning yourself to expect more. For the next five years I was blighted by them to varying degrees. I especially hated going into meetings, plays, shows, meals out, haircuts, dentist visits or pretty much anything in public, scared that I would shout something out or lose control. I still managed to get married, be best man twice, have children, and even play in a rock band (apparently, the reason I could do that was because I was effectively being somebody else on stage). I avoided nothing important and missed out on very little, except the pleasure that I should have felt at a lot of events where, instead, I experienced mainly dread in the hours, days, weeks or even months leading up to them.

So when Manda became pregnant I was determined to get myself fixed. I went to see a GP who referred me to the local mental health team, which sounds scary when you read that on a piece of paper with your name on it. And without needing to resort to medication of any kind, I underwent a course of cognitive behavioral therapy with a clinical psychologist. Essentially, she taught me to constantly put myself in situations that I found stressful and sit through the panic. Do it often enough so it becomes habitual, and the anxiety disappears.

It had a positive effect for a couple of years after the boys were born. I stopped work to look after them full-time once Manda's maternity leave finished (I've remained self-employed ever since) and I was pretty much back to how I had been before anxiety. So we went to playgroups, and swimming lessons, and health checks, and libraries. Essentially all the stuff — and possibly more — that any other children would go to. I still wasn't a fan of meetings but I saw that as a positive. Meetings, in my experience, tend to be elongated opportunities for people who don't really do anything to decide — at great length — how to completely upset the lives of people who do do things. I am convinced that nothing good has ever come out of a meeting.

But then the episodes of panic came back.

I was writing a piece about a specialist bike-fitting company and they had brought in a special bike rig to show me. This machine could alter its shape and size as you sat on it, so the top tube could get longer, or the seat tube, all controlled by a laptop. I was sitting on this thing testing it out, with a whole lot of people watching, and I suddenly started worrying that I was going to wee myself. In the end, I had to get off the bike and go to the loo just to check I was OK. But by then the seed was resown. I have tried to use the CBT techniques we employed to combat it first time, but I haven't quite managed to master it. Were I now to get a jury service letter, forced to go on a speed awareness course or have an agonising toothache, I'd be bricking it.

However, one thing that does help — a lot — is just getting out on the bike. In fact, I can quite happily do ride stories or interview someone while cycling alongside them without any fear. As with the hypochondria, I'm sort of hoping this awesome jaunt through France might just give me a figurative shot in the arm to be a bit braver.

Excuse the forced segue here, but our choice to go freestyling on this route has certainly given our morale a shot in the arm and we phone mum and Manda from a strange, tiny chapel set at the confluence of three roads just outside Le Voide. With a bright and clear sky, not too much heat, and our goal for the day at Argenton well within reach, all is well with the world. Then we look in the window of the old chapel. Inside there's nothing but neat scaffolding, some road signs, and a single chair placed right in the middle of the concrete floor. It is, quite obviously, an interrogation chamber. We reapply our sunspray and quickly scoot off.

The last big town on our route today is Vihiers and we soon arrive in the centre. My chain slipped off the bottom of the cassette on the way here, so dad gets his tools out — oo-er — and gives the rear mech a tweak. Vihiers, seemingly as with the rest of France outside of the established tourist traps, could generously be described as sleepy. Although you'd probably need to put your ear to its chest just to confirm that. There's nothing really open save for a couple of tabacs and, curiously, a lingerie shop. C'est la France.

Vihiers is also the point where we rejoin the established route, so it's back onto another awful 'D' road south towards Argenton. A few miles into this slog

I get the hump (I could have said 'the arse-ache', but that's been happening all day) and decide to branch off left into some rural roads with small villages that might — only might, mind — have a shop open where we can get something for dinner. As we enjoy the peace and quiet of these country lanes a Mirage fighter jet blasts overhead, not more than a few hundred feet above us. I'm tempted to say, if the French put as much money into loo paper as they do into warmongering they might have a decent country on their hands. That's a bit unfair, we've been all right for loo paper on this trip. But from what we've seen of the country so far, it's incredible it still has a strong enough economy to support a modern military.

The first village we come to, Saint Paul du Bois, has a little English-style corner shop — or 'mini-mart', to use an Americanism that both us and the French can enjoy sharing a dislike for. We stock up on goat saucisson and Laughing Cow cheese, but there's no cider. We buy a couple of large plastic bottles of Saint Omer lager instead. The strange man in the shop — truly a local fellow for local people — doesn't have any bread, although he tells us to try the boulangerie up the road. After a bit of looking round, we discover the boulangerie of which he speaks is closed. Quelle surprise.

Keeping to the backroads, we get a little lost, and I'm constantly having to refer to the map app on my phone to check where we are. There are some pretty sights, though, and dad enjoys whipping out his camera at moments of interest.

I'm happy to take Matt's advice when it comes to our route and since leaving Chalonnes he's taken us on a turn for the better, away from the main road and into rural lanes. There is an abundance of vines beside the roadside. On our last visit, I remember the route being a rapid succession of different crops as we journeyed south, and that it was possible to roughly gauge where we were by the things that grew either side of the road. We now ride on country roads that thankfully lack the motorised urgency of the 'D' roads, so are much nicer to experience. In an effort to get off the busy roads, we detour into the countryside.

It is very pleasant but Matt feels we are taking a much longer route towards Argenton. He may well be right, but aside from the ever present thirst and hunger, it is not a major problem.

We get back on a busier road that heads straight for our campsite at Argenton. Like most other French roads we've been on so far, it is as straight as an arrow. It is on the last straight push towards the town that we overtake a fellow cyclist, clearly another cycle tourist with bags fore and aft, and who has that well-worn look of a rider and bike who has been on the road for quite some time. We greet him in French, although Matt suspects from his Altura panniers that he's probably English.

We descend into Argenton, it looks familiar, then up the hill towards the campsite. Matt hops off the bike trying to find somewhere we can buy bread, and I wait on the campsite road. Within minutes, the rider we just passed joins me. He has that bonhomie that is evoked by the sight of a fellow cycle tourist. We exchange the usual pleasantries, he is on his way to Montpellier, something that he has done regularly before by the sound of it. His bike is an amalgamation of numerous parts, all of some quality and all very much cyclo-tourist.

(Warning: the next paragraph is for cycling touring buffs only.)

His T.J.Quick frame is made from Reynolds 531 tubing. It is a longish wheelbase frame fitted with Campagnolo caliper brakes, despite there being brazed-on mountings for the more powerful cantilever brakes. He tells me that he bought this frame cheaply when his last frame broke, and that it was a less expensive alternative to having his original frame repaired. He has Campagnolo gear levers fitted on the down tube and his chainset is a classic TA Cyclo Tourist with two chainrings. Naturally he has a Brooks leather saddle that glows with the shape and patina that only years of use can produce.

As we speak, Matt returns and as usual his bike comes under scrutiny. One thing our new friend notices straightaway is the brand new Brooks B17 leather saddle. He rightly thinks it could be a problem on a trip of this length. Our chum goes for groceries while Matt and I go to the campsite.

Argenton is in a valley, so we drop down, cross the river, then face a short sharp climb up the other side to the campsite. Before we reach it, though, we stop. Dad still doesn't seem fussed about food but I'm seriously not keen to go another night with substandard nosh. At the very least we must have bread. I can't find any here right now but I do pop into a pharmacy to buy a chapstick. Both dad's and my lips are blistering in the sun. Of course, it's only one of a litany of ailments we're suffering but it's one that can be easily fixed. The nice lady in the pharmacy helpfully understands what I want and gets it for me.

By the time I get back to dad he's found a little friend: the cycle tourist we passed earlier. For the purposes of this, we'll call him Keith. Keith has been here before and — like a good stereotypical British cycle tourist — he knows a lot about a lot and drops the occasional French phrase into each sentence. Helpfully, Keith tells us there's a little supermarket up the road.

That's great, I'll go later. I'm prevented from going now by my paranoid android companion. After the slight confusion when we arrived officially after hours at last night's germ-warfare-unit-come-campsite, dad seems to be convinced we must get to every overnight stop in good time. He insists we head down the road and sign in first. So we do, and it's another flashback moment — where I dozed off and then had my very first taste of ice tea 21 years ago. We register at reception and dad's pleased because the campsite has free Wifi. I'm still thinking more about what I consider to be a fundamental requirement: food.

I unload the bike and leave dad to put up the tent while I go searching for Keith's fabled 'supermarché'.

At this point you may be thinking: how can he leave his 63-year-old dad to put up the tent while he goes looking for food? Let me tell you, considering the condition of my arse, I am really not taking the soft option. In any case, considering the form dad's been in on this trip, he's liable to come back with rubber gloves, industrial cleaner and a toilet brush rather than anything we can actually eat.

I find the supermarket quite quickly and it's a real beauty. Our friend Keith is in there as well. I go crazy picking us plenty of good grub: crisps, bread, Orangina, and some soft strawberry sweets that Adam requested before I left Jersey. I get the old chap some tartelettes amandine, as I know almonds are one of the few things he can actually taste. Hallelujah! We shall eat like kings. I also buy some more shower gel and, crucially, some cotton wool pads to try and protect my sore parts.

Keith is waiting outside the shop and wants a chat. That's fine. Then he says he's off to a bar for a beer before setting up camp. That's fine, too. I let him go on his way and I skedaddle back to the campsite. It's a bustling venue with lots of families. Behind a row of bushes I can hear the sound of children enjoying a swimming pool. Dad's put up the tent in the shade of a tree, so we unpack and I then face the challenge of hitting the shower. As with our first two campsites the facilities are really clean, and unlike our last cycle tour here, the French seem to have fully embraced the notion of sitting down to take a dump rather than having to aim it like an RAF bomber through a hole in the floor.

Those little luxuries count for nothing as I treat my afflicted parts, though. I always thought there would be a 'men in prison' element to this trip, but the idea I would feel excruciating pain while bending over in the shower wasn't quite what I had in mind. I have to go through this to keep the area clean, though, and now I can at least cushion and protect the damaged skin with the cotton wool pads I've just bought. Although tempted, I decided not to go for a swim — if the sight of the pad in my shorts is anything to go by, I'd look like a member of the Red Arrows leaving a trail through the water.

As I stroll back to the tent I see Keith coming the other way. He's saying something to dad, dad's saying something back. It all has the façade of good-natured behaviour, but I detect a certain iciness. I think I can imagine what's happened.

I ask dad what's afoot.

"He was going to put his tent up next to ours. The lady at the campsite office told him to, but he's put it over there now," dad says, almost too innocently.

"Oh yes, why was that?" I ask.

"Oh, I don't know. I don't think I was rude or anything but I was busy so he went to pitch over there instead."

"So what did you say?"

"Nothing. Oh, I can't remember," dad says, perfecting the old person's ability to forget stuff almost instantly. "But anyway, I could see him wanting to join in with our grub. He also said he was quite noisy at night."

I'm not hugely sociable at the best of times, much less when I'm hundreds of miles from home and in agony, so the idea of having a random stranger share in my despair doesn't really appeal to me either. I'm just intrigued to know how rude dad had to be to accomplish this.

"Fair enough," I say. "I wonder what noises he makes?"

"I don't know," dad replies. "Maybe he's a bit funny or something."

Being a bit "funny" in dad's lexicon really could mean anything.

After the mandatory shower and clothes washing, we tuck into our spread of bread, cheese, brioches, biscuits and beer. We eat alone, although our new friend made some overtures towards joining us. I can't remember exactly what I said to him (...or do I?).

This is the first campsite we've come to that has a Wifi provision, although it's only in a limited area around the reception office. I head off to try to use my tablet and perhaps post something on Facebook. I am very far from a technical expert but the campsite's Wifi is so slow that pigeon post looks a viable alternative. It's forced me to abandon any ideas of blogging or sending out interesting information as we progress on this trip. I can't do any justice to the fast-moving world of social media with connections as slow as these — by the time I tweet that I had ice in my coke, it would have melted.

However, overall I feel in pretty good shape. It's been a good day, and we're back on schedule.

We quite easily forget about Keith — even though he is only sitting about 50 yards behind us looking forlorn — and eat our first proper cycle touring dinner. We really enjoy it all and have a good chat, too. Dad says he can't taste the almond cake but thanks me for trying. After dinner I take our water bottles and give them a good going over with our Fairy Liquid. We also wash our clothes in what I hope is non-Legionella water.

Despite the raging pain I'm feeling, we're both pretty contented with the day's events. I think we should both still eat and drink more en route — I reckon that's why I'm flagging in the last 10 miles — but that could equally be psychological, knowing that we're almost done for the day.

We speak to mum and Manda before bed, then I start planning our route for tomorrow. If the weather forecast is right, it could be a tough day.

Day 3 — Health Matters

RIDES OF PASSAGE

DAY 4
On Your Bike

**Wednesday August 17, 1994 — Argenton les Vallées
to Chauvigny (70 miles)
Wednesday August 5, 2015 — Argenton les Vallées
to Chasseneuil du Poitou (55.5 miles)**

Matt aged 15

I managed to actually have a good night's sleep using Dad's sleeping mat. We woke up at around 6am but it was dark so we got up at 6.30am. By 7.30am we had packed away all our gear, Dad taking my share of the tent. We set off quickly, eager to cover the ground we were short from yesterday.

After the descent leaving the camp we had a long climb. This eventually led to Massais then on to Thouars. Here Dad bought some cakes and I ate a peach and some choccy. We left Thouars down what we thought was the right road. We ended up in front of a huge château then in a little town, which we did not aim for. Anyhow, after losing three quarters of an hour we got the right road.

This led us to Taizé (where we bought water), Saint Jouin and Marnes. By now I was pulling away from Dad on the hills as he had a knee problem. We stopped in Jaunay-Clan near Futuroscope and went to find something to eat - a lager and a ham sandwich. We left the town at 2.30pm and had already done 80km.

On the way out we passed Futuroscope and its associated hotels and headed for Chasseneuil - a huge industrial estate. We left Chasseneuil but could not find the D20, the road we should take. We decided the route given was rubbish.

Dad asked a woman the way and we eventually made progress. Dad was struggling quite a bit now but we managed to get through a load of lanes to the N151. This was a very busy road and took us right into Chauvigny.

We stopped in the town centre to buy food. We bought bread, drinks, red wine, pâté, saucisson and pizza. We then headed for the campsite. It was quite close. We had a shower and did a load of washing. We then had our food. The place is full of Germans.

We went to phone Mum with a new phone card Dad bought in Lavaux. Afterwards we went to bed after hanging our washing to dry inside (!) the tent.

We rode really well, really quickly today but Dad's knee is playing up.

We travelled 118.3km today.

Arthur aged 42

Decided to carry all the tent on my bike so that Matthew would not struggle too much. Indeed, he went well today, without any of the grovelling or hill walking of previous days. Today it was me who struggled. My bad knee of yesterday got gradually worse and climbing or riding into wind was a problem.

Fortunately Matt did not drop me as I seem to freewheel a lot better, either due to my better hubs or my superior weight. A good day's cycling with some 'through and off' going on.

Got into Chauvigny at 15.55 hrs, which must be a record, despite getting lost a bit around Futuroscope. No Tour de France road writing today, but saw a cow asleep against a haystack on the way out of Argenton.

Highlights of the day:
— The campsite is good.

Matt aged 36

Up before 7am again today, the plan being to get some good miles in before the heat comes. According to the weather apps on my phone, we're looking at temperatures well over 30 degrees Celsius later and we've got a fair way to ride if we're going to reach Chauvigny. I'm not exactly feeling in tip-top form, although today it's only aches and pains, no little surprises about life-threatening water-borne diseases.

I go to the showers and treat those parts that need to be treated. I'm now using Savlon Healing Gel down there, with a doubled-up cotton wool pad acting as a cushion. But it's still complete agony. I can hardly bend down to pull out the tent pegs ('pulling out the tent pegs' isn't a euphemism, by the way) and God knows what I look like while walking. The showers are being cleaned and have a disinfectant smell that reminds me of my primary school. It's funny how smells can be so evocative. I never really liked having to go to primary or secondary school — although my nursery school was wonderful — so this aroma hardly inspires cheeriness.

I'm a bit tired, too. Before we came over, mum said to me: "You'll sleep well, not having to worry about the boys' school, or work, or moving house. You can just concentrate on cycling."

It's true that I'm not really thinking about those domestic issues — although I am noticing the emails that come through every time I switch data roaming on my phone to consult Google Maps — but I've now got other problems to solve. Like, can we find a route that doesn't involve dicing with traffic on busy regional roads? How many hills are there? How much pain can I take? And why am I not sleeping?

Before we leave I also surreptitiously do something that I'm probably not allowed to. I have brought a little Trangia mini stove and a litre of meths with us for a brew up. But a cup of tea has been the last thing on our minds so far on this trip and I need to start making life easier for myself. So I sneakily go to the loos and pour the meths away. I'm not sure that's allowed but it's done now.

It's a cool, overcast morning and our friend Keith is up and packed before us. Dad marvels at his speed. He comes over and wishes us well — very sporting considering the old chap's cold shoulder last night.

There have been more bells here and again their peels seem to make no sense, but by now I don't care. More interesting is the buzz of a microlight overhead. I'm sure it's a great view, but it's only just after 7am. What time must the pilot have got up, purely to act like a human mosquito and irritate everybody else on the ground? Perhaps he's flying to his shop, which he'll open at 8am and remain serving behind the counter until 6pm. But, c'est la France, so I very much doubt it.

By 7.55 we're in the saddle. Well, I'm standing on the pedals — every time I lower myself onto the saddle, sharp needles of pain burst up through me. I really don't know if I can do this much more.

Our planned course this morning effectively cuts a corner from our original route and has the added bonus of — hopefully — using quiet rural roads. The aim when we decided to do this trip was to follow our original itinerary as closely as possible, but French roads have got a lot busier in the 21 years since then. Drivers still give cyclists a wide berth, but neither of us wants to be mixing with traffic the whole way across a country.

Today we also have a new problem. Dad's GPS tracker's memory is down to less than 50 per cent so there's no way it'll record the whole trip. I do have my two Strava and Garmin systems working as well, but I can appreciate why dad would want his own. He says his machine has a MicroSD card slot in it, though, so I presume that's for added memory. Before leaving Argenton completely, I decide we should detour to last night's supermarket. I take the initiative and go in to ask for the MicroSD in my stilted French, but to no avail. They only have full-size SD cards here.

Arthur aged 63

After the usual disembarkation business, we set off again just after 08.00hrs. Keith has already broken camp and headed off way before us. As he passed he said 'au revoir', and was gone. His words were a mix of English and French. I'm not sure why he did this, but it kept me on my toes.

Part of the reason for his speedy getaway was that he had a minute one-person, one-position-only tent which let him lie down and that's all. It was probably sufficient for him but would have been way too small for us. The necessity for a larger tent becomes very apparent this morning, because I needed five attempts to put my bib-shorts on correctly. Without going into great detail, it is hard to explain the exact difficulties, but I would never have been able to put them on within the confines of anything smaller.

With the impending failure of my GPS to hold much more of our route, we go in search of another MicroSD card. Matt has no luck, but he does buy food, which is always welcome. We take a different route out of Argenton, so no sleeping cows on this occasion.

We start pedalling in earnest. Now we truly are on the road. In any other circumstances it would be the perfect conditions for an early morning spin: the air is cool; there's a very slight mist; and the surrounding farmland is largely flat and green. But I'm getting towards the end of my pain threshold.

How did I reach this point? Why did I feel it would be OK to use a brand new Brooks saddle on a 600-mile cycle tour?

The truth is a fair few people told me I'd have to break the saddle in — I knew it myself already anyway — but the contrary side of my character rather came to the fore. Also, when it comes to bikes, there's never any shortage of advice from all sorts of quarters. I'd even go so far as to suggest there are more pompous know-alls in cycling than any other pastime. But maybe I have that opinion just because I've been so close to cycling for so long. The funny thing is, no matter how simple bikes are, and no matter how much people know about them, or how certain they seem about their ideas and opinions, most people are still winging it and don't really understand quite why some things happen.

How can I make such a sweeping statement? Because I know of only two people whose opinion I will instantly allow to override my own. The first is the old chap, but I've seen him plenty foxed by an unhelpful bike in the past. The second is Mike Burrows, the greatest bike designer in history and a genuine natural genius. But even Mike will tell you he doesn't know everything.

I first came into contact with Mike when I was asked to write an obituary for Richard Ballantine in *Cycling Weekly*. Even though Mike and the cycling media have had a fractious relationship in the past, and he didn't know me from Adam, we spent an hour chatting on the phone. Then we spoke again a few weeks later, and again the following month. And every month or two since we've ended up chatting mainly about bikes.

If you're a cyclist, you might already know who Burrows is but here's a quick résumé. Mike created the very first carbon monocoque bicycle, which became the Lotus bike that Chris Boardman rode to Olympic glory in 1992. Mike then became chief designer for Giant Bicycles — the world's biggest bike manufacturer — where he created the TCR, or 'Compact Road' frame, with its innovative sloping top tube. Look at road bikes now and you'll see that almost all of them have sloping top tubes — Burrows's Giant TCR was the first. He invented the 'Speedy' or 'Windcheetah' recumbent bike. He invented the 8Freight long-wheel base transporter bike. He pioneered the monoblade fork, which led to the Cannondale Lefty front suspension fork. He even invented the in-line or barrel adjuster — the little knob found on gear cables that you twist to fine tune the accuracy of gear shifting.

My favourite story about Mike actually happened quite recently. He went out for a training ride on his racing recumbent — an ultra-efficient bike design where you lie back rather than sit upright in the saddle — and stopped to chat to a couple of chaps on their 'normal' road bikes. They were new cyclists and they stared in wonder at the amazing contraption he was riding, asking Mike all sorts of questions. Eventually Mike said to them: "You know, I invented this bike I'm riding."

They looked at him incredulously, barely believing him.

They believed him even less when he pointed to their two compact road bike frames and said: "And I invented your bikes, too."

The funny thing about Mike is that, even though he answers to nobody when it comes to bicycle knowledge, he's actually one of the least pompous bike experts I've met. If you're willing to listen and ask questions, he's happy to explain everything.

He hasn't normally got much time for bike reviewers, though, because we're always using dodgy reasoning to explain what we feel when we write tests. He also hates the PR nonsense that comes from bike companies, which people like me also use to excuse the newest bit of, often ineffectual, bike design or technology. Essentially Mike thinks that bikes can feel different, but it's sometimes very hard to reason why they feel like that. And if Mike Burrows says sometimes it's hard to understand why a bike feels the way it does, you should probably be a little skeptical of anybody who says with complete certainty they do know exactly why.

In my world I can put dad alongside Mike because I've seen him at first-hand tweaking and fettling more people's bikes, including my own, than anybody else. He does a great job of fixing things. And when we arrive at our first town today, Moutiers sous Argenton, he fixes my bike in a supremely selfless way.

"Do you want to swap saddles?" the old chap asks.

In any other situation I would have said no. This has been my mistake, I should live with it. Also, taking it will reinforce that old sensation of me being the son and dad being the father again, even at the respective ages of 36 and 63. I realise dad's done most of the French talking on this trip, too, with me like a not-so-junior sidekick. Essentially, I feel like I've become a child again.

I'll try to change the other aspects of that but I'm really grovelling physically, so I'm going to have to take his saddle. I'm not that proud.

Not only is dad's Brooks saddle already broken in and bum shaped, but it's a bit thinner than the model I have on my bike. A lot of the pain I'm suffering is originating in the crevice between leg and groin, no doubt caused by my frankly fat thighs. Dad has got a bum of steel and much thinner legs than me so there's a fair chance he'll get away with the wider seat. He's also wearing some excellent bibshorts I've bought him — normally he rides his bike without padding of any kind. I tell him that if my saddle starts to give him gyp, though, we'll swap back. There's no need for two of us to be in pain.

As Matt is still suffering with the results of a prolonged period on a brand new saddle, when we reach Moutiers sur Argenton I very gamely offer him the opportunity to swap seats. Because both seatposts are the same size, it is simply a case of undoing the seat bolt and swopping the whole saddle and seatpost over from one bike to the other. The only thing to be careful about is tightening the seat bolt. These are generally made from some cheesy material, so we have to be gentle when we do the bolt up.

The good news is that because my saddle is narrower and run-in, it is instantly more comfortable for Matt. I pray that the sculpted padding of my British-made Lusso shorts will protect me from the aggressive contours of a brand new leather Brooks. The shorts have certainly worked brilliantly so far on this trip.

Our route follows 'D' roads that run as straight as an arrow and the countryside is reassuringly flat. We cycle between two fields that contain hundreds of pigs — it is like a full English Breakfast on the hoof. While taking photos, the pigs on our side of the road start raising their snouts and sniffing the air. When we turn around, the reason is obvious: their buddies on the far side are getting fed and the smell of whatever it is, is driving them wild. The squealing noises are quite unbelievable.

We leave before a porcine revolution breaks out.

The route gets flatter and the countryside opens up for miles around, only broken by the inevitable wind farm, a water tower or sometimes a château.

We stop for another MicroSD card hunt at Saint Verant, where we also have breakfast. The roundabout facing us is decorated with bunting and has three flag poles with two bicycles attached to each. We sit by the war memorial and munch our pains aux raisins. Sadly no MicroSD cards in Saint Verant, or in our next town Airvault. But at least here I manage to buy bread, water and pure pork saucisson.

Using dad's saddle, my discomfort certainly doesn't fade away instantly but I can sense it's not getting any worse, which is a start. We make good time and stop at Airvault, possibly the oddest-named town on our trip yet. It sounds like a kids' sci-fi film. After posing for a picture on a bridge over the river, we head down into the town centre.

Airvault marks the beginning of the transition between the grey slate tile roofs of northern France and the red tile roofs of southern France. There's a fair mixture of both here. We refer to a large town map display to get our bearings but I just can't make head nor tail of it. Is my Legionnaires' disease finally taking hold and this is the early onset of the promised confusion? No fear, I see what's happening. This map has been drawn south-north rather than north-south, so everything is essentially back to front.

I'm starting to tire of French eccentricities.

We continue into the town centre and dad pops into a boulangerie to buy bread for tonight, in case we can't find anywhere else en route. I think he's getting the message about grub. While he's inside I hear two English people chatting as they climb into a French-registered Toyota Prius. I could almost hug them and have to stop myself from saying: "Hello there, I speak English, too. Would you like to talk to me?" But soon they're inside the car and gone. Meanwhile, behind me, a noisy local family is either playing, or fighting, or play-fighting out of sight beyond some open French windows. (Or should that be some open French French windows?)

Dad and I climb up out of Airvault and find ourselves on a huge, expansive plain, full of wide arable fields. I know we're not that high in terms of true altitude but it really seems like there's nothing between us and God up here. You almost feel the need to duck so as not to bang your head on the sky. Ironically, there aren't any churches in sight, though. Obviously faith alone won't bring a decent harvest. Will God provide? Seems like the locals round here might be hedging their bets.

The climb out of Airvault is relatively short and soon we're riding between endless, flat fields that stretch to the horizon. It's not easy or particularly pleasant riding country but even with a headwind it is quick. My bike is going well.

I have to admit that I am something of a born-again bicycle rider. I had rarely given the bicycle any thought at all from the age of 15 until I started working at the bike shop aged 29. In my teens, especially when I was nearing the age when I was able to drive a car, it was desperately uncool to cycle anywhere unless you were some kind of saddo or slightly unhinged. I probably fit both those descriptions, but nevertheless I did the only thing left to me, and that was to walk. That was also not very cool but it did suggest that maybe my car was at the menders, or more likely wrapped around a tree. Even this was better than admitting I used a bicycle.

Also, as a fashion statement, I wore driving gloves and slip-on driving shoes. They both seemed quite cool in an understated way — remember, we're talking about the very late 1960s/early 1970s here — and frankly, at that age I grasped at any straw that might be slightly avante-garde. The trouble with both these garments was that while they were perfect for someone who spent a lot of their time inside a motor car, they were totally useless to someone who generally walked everywhere. The shoes let the rain in and the driving gloves, with all those holes, gave no protection against the cold.

By the time I was nearly 18, I had a job and was able to buy my own car. No longer was I dependant on the generosity of friends and relations to move around and I could go where I wanted, whenever I wanted. Remarkably, I never crashed my first set of wheels — more by luck than judgment — and went on to have a range of cars that reached its pinnacle with a Lotus 7, which I raced at the Bouley Bay hill-climb in Jersey.

That is quite a long way from bikes, you may think, but I have also raced a bicycle at Bouley Bay. At both events it's you on your own against the clock, and in a strange way it quite clearly underlines what a great invention the bicycle is. Forty years ago I drove a sports car that weighed 6cwt, powered by an engine that gave a modest 140 horsepower. My fastest time at Bouley Bay was 51.20 seconds. Some years afterwards, I cycled a racing bike up the same course and I did it in 157 seconds. That's slightly more than three times slower but it's using a human engine that develops only a quarter of a horsepower or less. What a great device the bicycle is. And this is before we work out the difference between a car and a bicycle in both initial purchase price and running costs. And before we throw in the environmental and health benefits of cycling, too.

My message to anyone — unless you are old and infirm, or you hate getting wet, or you have a huge distance to cover in a short time — is try a bike. Not only will you get fitter but you will be more aware of your surroundings, you'll produce less greenhouse gas (Matt would say that's arguable in my case) and it will cost you a lot less as well. This is why I adore bicycles and why they make such a good form of transport.

When you want to fully absorb any country that you are travelling through, the bike is perfect. From a saddle you can see, hear and smell more of what is there. And because almost everyone has had a bike at some time, they present some common ground that you can share with the people you meet.

Having said that, I find it interesting that people recognise the difference between a Mercedes and a Ford, yet don't realise, or even refuse to realise, that there are big differences between bicycles. But there are some fairly obvious distinctions. For example, possibly the most popular type of bike is the hybrid, trekking or city bike. These are a popular general-purpose choice for the typical man or woman. They have an upright riding position, lots of simple-to-use gears, powerful brakes, and are easy and comfortable to ride.

Then there are mountain bikes that everyone has heard of. In many ways they saved the bicycle industry because they were trendy, so they created an interest in cycling among a wider audience. Early mountain bikes had wide, flat handlebars, powerful cantilever brakes, wide tyres, low gears and offered a very stable ride. They were easy to sell to most would-be cyclists, who were normally put off by road bikes' drop handlebars, narrow tyres, and gears that often forced you to walk up certain hills. Today, since the arrival of hybrid bikes, mountain bikes have become sportier and more specific to whatever off-road purpose you plan to use them for.

Ironically, drop-bar road or 'racing' bicycles have seen a massive resurgence in their popularity in recent years. That's partly been down to sportive mass participation cycle events, and partly due to British cycling successes at the Tour de France and Olympics. A road bike needs less effort to pedal, but can also be less comfortable to ride than other bikes. This is because it has thin tyres that are often pumped up to 100psi or more, a short wheelbase which means it is very stiff and responsive, and close-ratio gears. You will go quickly on a road bike but you will also feel every bump in the tarmac and the ride is lively. You might find this quite unnerving until you get used to it, and you may walk up the steeper hills.

None of this actually concerns me and Matt right now because we are on touring bikes. For many young scorchers, touring bikes are the final step in a downward spiral, but they are surprisingly popular for everyday use among the more experienced. Why is this? They are usually made from a high-quality frame material such as top-grade steel or titanium, which is light and also forgiving. The frame angles are not too steep, so they still go swiftly but not at the expense of comfort. They have powerful mountain bike type cantilever or disc brakes, so they can stop quickly with or without luggage attached. They have a wide range of gear ratios, which means that hills never pose a problem. Then they have dropped handlebars so that the rider has the option of four or more hand positions. To round off the practicality stakes, they usually have pannier racks and mudguards fitted. Why struggle under the weight of a rucksack when the bike can carry all that and probably more? And do cycle in the rain by all means, but why have a muddy stripe up your back and dirt all over the bike?

Rain, however, is the least of our worries right now as we head nearer towards the outskirts of Poitiers.

It's hot again and there's a fierce headwind once more, but I take the front and we really go well, knocking out five miles in about 15 minutes — a record on this trip. On the way we see a sign for a donkey race, which seems strangely apt. I keep looking ahead, hoping to spot some kind of landmark in the distance, but it really does seem as if we're getting nowhere, albeit nowhere quickly.

The road, a grey thread through a calm sea of yellow and green, is reasonably busy but it joins up with a far bigger dual carriageway on the outskirts of Poitiers. Avoiding this, we follow a back route to get us to our planned lunch stop in Neuville. It's a fairly industrial area around here, although Neuville centre ville is quite pretty. We park up and, making good on my earlier resolution, I decide to go into a charming little boulangerie-patisserie to buy lunch. There are all sorts of chocolate and cake-based delicacies in here. At any other time I would have thought I had gone to heaven but for lunch we really need stodge — a sandwich or something similar. I have a very awkward conversation with the girl behind the counter, but I at least get a decent meal out of it: two croque-monsieurs and two coffee eclairs, all wrapped beautifully.

We find some shade on a bench in the centre of the square and eat. Dad takes the opportunity to snap some photos of the impressive Hôtel de la Ville while I top up my Garmin with some charge from the power bank emergency battery I've brought with me. We're starting to realise our power supplies might not last the whole trip. My hub-mounted dynamo, apart from sounding awful and driving me crazy with its incessant click-click noise, is doing its best to recharge my phone, but I'm still having to top that up with the power bank each night, too. At this rate, if dad's GPS ends up out of action, I'm going to have to decide whether to use the Garmin or just my phone and consolidate the power into one device. I'll think about it later. For now, the biggest problem is that sun beating down — it's the hottest it's been all trip, which is really saying something.

We get back on the bikes but I don't feel refreshed. It takes a while to reseat my bum in a position that I can just about live with. As we head out of Neuville we pass through some incredible industrial areas, many run-down but still bearing great edifices of what they once were. A huge dilapidated warehouse towers over us and I take a photo. Because we're on the edge of Poitiers, heading towards the technology centre at Futuroscope, the roads around here are large. But according to the map, the route we'll be taking seems to have a bike path alongside it, so we should be safe.

Sure enough we find it. The cycle path itself is smooth and separated from the carriageway by some small trees. It's probably fine if you're a local commuter, but after a long day in the saddle already, I'm not enamoured by its rolling nature. This is supposed to be a relatively flat area, yet the way seems to be constantly going up and down. Compared to the blast we did earlier, where we made good time even with the wind in our faces, this is far harder. The old chap is going well, but I can feel blood and serum sticking my shorts to my bottom and legs.

Did we really come this way last time? According to my old diary we must have done. I thought I had a pretty clear memory of the Futuroscope day, but all I can remember are flat roads with big ditches at the side. If only my bike could talk we'd have a better idea.

I'm riding my Dawes Galaxy: exactly the same bike I used in 1994, with the same 21-year-old CTC sticker on the seat tube. Well, it's not *exactly* the same — it's undergone a thorough overhaul in the last month or so. With my romantic head on, I rather liked the idea of using the original bike to recreate the journey. In the support of effective and ageless technology, I thought it would strike a blow for the materialistic desire that new is always better. And with my hugely cynical cycling journalist's head on, I thought I might be able to sell the story of using a 21-year-old bike to ride across France to a bike mag.

So how do you make a 21-year-old touring bike tour-worthy again.

Let's start with the part that affected me most in 1994. On our last ride across France I suffered from a bad back, primarily because the bike was too short for me. I've ridden my Galaxy a lot since then but never for more than one day at a time. So I've never needed to really fix the problem of its reach not being long enough, and a slightly small frame tends to be more fun to ride in short blasts. But I knew I was going to need a more comfortable position on this trip — I needed a longer stem.

That's an easy thing to fix on modern bikes, which come with 'aheadset' stems. But my bike comes from the age of quill stems, and these days it's pretty hard to find the 130mm quill stem that I needed to stretch me out comfortably. That meant I had to fit a quill-to-aheadset converter. And if I was replacing the stem, I figured I might as well replace the old handlebars which, although very pretty, are too narrow for me.

That got my position sorted but there were also a lot of moving parts on my bike that I feared wouldn't stand the test of this challenge. The first were the wheels, which needed a few spokes replaced back in 1994 and were looking decidedly tired. So I ordered a great value set of wheels from M:Parts which came with Shimano Deore hubs and Mavic rims. With a total price of well under £200 for both wheels, they were a bargain.

To these I fitted Schwalbe Marathon Plus tyres with ultra puncture protection. Before we set off some people suggested that these tyres would be overkill and wouldn't supply enough ride 'feel'. But I don't think those people quite understood the nature of the challenge we faced. I'm quite happy to forego any amount of feel — in fact, the way I'm feeling right now, the less feel the better — if it means we can be puncture-free throughout.

Then to the drivetrain: chain, chainset, cassette and derailleurs. A new chain was a given but for that to work without fault I'd also need a new cassette (the block of rings or sprockets at the back wheel) and either new chainrings or a completely new chainset (the bit which the pedals are attached to). And here's where things get a bit tricky, because as time marches on, component manufacturers bring out new systems with more 'speeds' or gear choices. My bike was originally a seven speed, that is to say, there were seven sprockets on the cassette at the back. But seven-speed equipment these days is very hard to find because it is effectively defunct.

If I was to upgrade to the modern standard — a 10-speed drivetrain — I'd probably also need new front and rear derailleurs. But my old ones work perfectly and I at least wanted some original ingredients aside from just the frame of my old bike. So I opted for eight-speed kit — a mild upgrade but one that my existing components could handle. I bought a 12-32-tooth eight-speed cassette made by SRAM, an eight-speed SRAM chain, and then a cheap Acera 42/32/22-tooth eight-speed triple chainset made by Shimano. That Acera chainset exactly matched the ratios I had on my old chainset, so it was effectively a straight swap.

Now, old-school touring men may well ask, why did you not just change the rings on your old chainset? It's a good question, and it's perfectly possible. But that gets more complicated still as you have to deal with BCD and PCD measurements, and it would have cost me more than £100. I felt it was quicker, easier and cheaper to fit a whole new chainset, especially as I was fitting a new bottom bracket (the component which goes through the bottom of your frame and on which your chainset spins) for security, too.

Brakes weren't an area of major concern. The cantilevers on my bike may not be super powerful but they're good enough, especially with some decent aftermarket replacement brake blocks. Then it was just a case of fitting new cables, new bar tape, and pannier racks. My one divergence from the accepted cycle touring way was to have only one front rack. I couldn't get another one past the dynamo on the right hand side of my front wheel. But because the left pannier bag only contains my sleeping bag and mat — with a combined weight of less than 1kg — while the dynamo weighs about 700g, there's no great handling issues due to being unbalanced. In any case, Burrows says cyclists can learn to ride around and adapt to most problems.

So it's not quite 'Trigger's broom' — at its heart this is the same bike I used in 1994. And it's certainly holding up better than I am. Both dad and I are starting to wonder how we managed to do this 21 years ago. Because we swapped saddles and seatposts earlier, I also have a new ailment: my hip is starting to play up. If I don't have my saddle at exactly the right height, my hip goes numb, and it's kicking in now.

Day 4 — On Your Bike

As we draw near to Poitiers it becomes apparent why this was such a brilliant area for battles during the Hundred Years War. Flashbacks from primary school history lessons enter my memory with tales of great British victories like Crecy and Poitiers — all stirring stuff when you are eight or nine years old. The area is table-top flat, and I imagine that military strategists of the period could plan their moves and see the ensuing results without even changing vantage points. It is like a wargamer's paradise, but the carnage would have been real.

At this point of the trip, I should give some balance to history, and mention one or two French victories. Children are never taught about heir nation's defeats, and rightly so, can you imagine the fall in morale if kids heard about national failures on a regular basis? But a couple of French victories can't do much harm. So how about the Battle of Montmuran in 1354 that preceded the Battle of Poitiers? Or the Battle of Castillon in 1453, the French victory that ended the 100 Years War? In fact, the English only won one or two more battles than the French did, and between 1429 and the end of the Hundred Years War in 1453, the French won every battle — all eight of them. Did I mention my ancestors were French? Allez les bleus.

We cycle along a handy traffic-free cycle path as we approach Poitiers, and eventually find what we assume to be another convenient cycletrack that goes towards the camping. But this track ends abruptly near nothing of any consequence and we are forced to climb a steep bank to get back on the road.

This hopping on and off the bike reminds me of when Matt and I used to race in the local mountain bike series, around the time we did our last trans-France ride. When I became a 'veteran' — which meant I wouldn't see 40 again — it was like being reborn. I'd entered an age group that had its own set of results. I was quite fit for an old man. And, as my age category was quite small, it was not difficult to be a hero. One of the benefits of being a veteran is that most old people have more sense than to go rushing across mud, over rocks and through brambles for fun on Sunday mornings.

Having said all that, I did give it my all, which usually resulted in me gasping for breath throughout the race. I suspect it might have something to do with me previously smoking 40 fags a day. I did not know it at the time but these desperate gasps for air also gave me a unique advantage. While I was struggling for breath, I gave little thought to the vast curtain of saliva that hung from my mouth and floated in the breeze like a sticky version of the kind of scarf worn by cads driving old British sports cars. It was a brave rival who overtook too closely lest they be caught in my web of phlegm.

On another occasion, we all lined up across a particularly muddy field for the metaphorical gun to go off. The starter shouted: 'Go!' and the whole body of competitors struggled to move anywhere in the thick mud. But I had a brainwave and was off the bike, running like a demon. After about 50 yards I realised that no one was passing me or even close by — which was unusual. I turned around to see a line of riders desperately trying to make some headway in the gloop. I burst into laughter and, by the time I'd recovered, they were up beside me and the race began in earnest.

I have also done a bit of road racing, although again I was not very brilliant. When the road went upwards, I usually went backwards. However, I was quite fond of the 10-lap criterium-style events that the bike club would put on at a local purpose-made cycling circuit. Amazingly enough I also once won a time trial, although it was a handicapped event, so some kind person must have given me a very generous allowance. The event started and finished at the local cycling club clubhouse, and at the finish there were lashings of fruit cake and that other roadie staple: weak tea. I was more than surprised when they read out my name as winner, but I took it as graciously as I possibly could, knowing that it was probably a mistake.

Most of my bike riding has been as a commuter. As a broad rule, I generally commute everywhere by bike. One thing that has never changed over the years is the amount of chimpanzees, also on bicycles, who feel the need to overtake you at all costs. By this I mean they will run red lights, duck in between cars, ride on the pavement or run over pedestrians (on a crossing). The most amusing common denominator is that they ride bikes that can be best described as absolute piles of poo and which could benefit from a splash of oil. A good clue as to an imminent overtake is the frantic squeaking noise that approaches you from behind. The saddest of these types are the ones who go so slowly that you are forced to overtake them, then suddenly take it as a personal insult and race past within yards. The one I remember most was the young blade who was so interested in checking that he'd gone past me, he didn't see the van door open in front of him.

We stop for a break and are passed on the cycle path by two road riders in full Lycra. The first, younger one doesn't reply to our hellos. The second, older one asks if we have a problem. Proof indeed that nationalities may change, but roadies stay the same.

By the time we catch sight of Futuroscope we're both feeling pretty goosed, so we decide we should camp at the municipal campsite in Chasseneuil. Before we can get there, though, we have to negotiate a succession of roundabouts and overbuilt hotels in the trumped up industrial park that sits around Futuroscope. Finally we pass through Chasseneuil's very small village centre and follow the signs to the camping, finding it behind a short fence, right next to the road. The old chap goes in to do the signing-in duties while I try to stand in some shade. It turns out we've got the last pitch available, but dad's not impressed at the price. I'm not impressed at the pitch's position — in the corner, two metres from the road, and in full glare of the sun. Beggars really cannot be choosers.

We park the bikes and quickly put up the tent and lay out the grub we've got. We could do with some more, so dad decides to walk back to the few shops we just passed to see about extra supplies and some cider. I lie behind the tent to get some shade. It is skin-fryingly hot. I try to text home only to find out I've run out of credit on my phone and my auto top-ups have stopped for some reason. That means I can't access the net, which is a problem that needs resolving. I can't text anybody to ask them to help. And I can't go on the web to add credit. We'll have to use dad's phone — which isn't able to ring anybody, but it can text — to contact mum.

We manage to get the last pitch in the municipal campsite of Chasseneuil du Poitou, albeit at the most expensive cost so far: €16. There is no shade, the main road is two yards behind us, and the 24-hour TGV goes past 100 yards in front of our pitch. But it does have a free swimming pool.

Notwithstanding all this, we set up and I go in search of liquid refreshments. We had seen what we thought were shops about 500 yards away so I retrace our steps. Yes, they are shops, but they do not sell food or drink. Across the road is quite an up-market wine shop, which I hope might have something suitable.

The lady inside is extremely helpful. I get the feeling that it might be her first day at work and she is trying very hard, especially as — being cider-less — she fell at the first hurdle. This is no problem at all, we move onto the pink fizzy wine, which qualifies as a close second. The effort that this lady puts into selling me only something to wash our dinner down is impressive. If I was dining with the most attractive woman in the world, with seduction on my mind, I could not do any better than to put my faith in her suggestions. However, I am only there to buy the fuel to get us through another day, so I purchase the most modestly-priced bottle of fizzy stuff that I can find. Full marks to the shop assistant, though, because her enthusiasm is not dampened one bit.

Dad returns to say there was nothing open except for a shop that only sold wine — it is 4.45pm after all and c'est la France. The woman there encouraged him to buy a bottle of pink fizzy stuff for £10.

He's not impressed again but worse is about to strike. We discover our exclusive pitch is situated on an ant hill, and the little feckers have got into our biscuits and brioches for tomorrow morning. The old fella is livid — I'm starting to notice he really doesn't like creepy crawlies — and he throws away the infested food in a fit of pique.

Then I ask him if he can text home and get Manda to put more credit on my phone. Peering over his glasses — his eyesight is incredibly poor — he makes a cackhanded mess of this request, infuriating himself in the process. Vexation hits a clear 10. Then he trips over the tent rope. Finally he completes his little performance by accidentally spraying the fizzy wine all over everything like a victorious Lewis Hamilton. Meanwhile, the traffic rumbles past six feet behind us and a TGV blasts through the station a hundred yards ahead. With dad hopping over guy lines, it really is all a strange dance between comedy and tragedy.

We begin to prepare dinner. This has spent some time on the floor and sadly it is infested with ants. I do wonder if that extortionate pitch cost was because we are paying by the ant. Then the expensive pink wine explodes all over me as I search for ant-free foodstuffs. These are in the minority. It is a major victory for the ants. We come away with some saucisson, the bread, some cheese, the tinned sardines and whatever pink wine that the ants are not holding a swimming gala in.

Eventually calmness is restored and I head to the showers for my evening ritual of pain and torture. Things are no better down there, so I reapply Healing Gel and a cotton wool pad and return to the tent. Dad goes for a wash and I decide to use this moment of privacy inside the tent to take selfies of my unmentionables in an attempt to see what's going on. To be honest, I can't really tell. But in the confines of this sweltering ripstop boil-in-the-bag coffin, the experience has certainly left me sweating. Unfortunately my phone's photos automatically upload to my computer back at home, so I'd better warn mum and Manda to prepare for what they might see on PhotoStream. Let's hope they're not checking our pictures each night around the dinner table.

Dad comes back and seems to be of the opinion that there are couples up to something naughty in the communal showers. I think that's very unlikely, although I did take a photo of two flies having it off on the outside of our tent earlier. But then it is called the flysheet. I expected them (the flies, that is) to buzz off as I closed in to take the shot but they must have been lost in the moment. C'est la France. Incidentally, both dad and I are firmly of the opinion that this country is a farce, a shambles.

I've also decided I don't like camping and I can't understand why the French do it en masse. It's like living in public with a whole load of new neighbours you have to meet and learn to despise instantly. I prefer my hatred to reach the right consistency after years of fermenting.

We have dinner, flicking ants off the bread and cheese, and using our fingers to eat sardines in tomato sauce (dad picked this unusual choice of finger food, need you wonder). We truly are living the high life.

So we didn't quite reach Chauvigny today, where we wanted to be, although at 33.3 degrees Celsius it was just far too hot. I can't see us catching up tomorrow either, but at least we're heading somewhere interesting: the Vienne Valley — dad's favourite bit from the 1994 tour.

We chat to mum and Manda on dad's phone. We have both perked up a bit after eating and recognise the ridiculousness of our situation. Secretly, though, I don't know if I can keep doing this. I plan tomorrow's route anyway.

Still perspiring in the tent at 10pm, we go to sleep.

Thought for the day: If England is a nation of shopkeepers, France is a nation of shop-owners (who never open).

RIDES OF PASSAGE

DAY 5
Island Life

Thursday August 18, 1994 — Chauvigny to Saint Junien (64 miles)
Thursday August 6, 2015 — Chasseneuil du Poitou to Confolens (62.5 miles)

Matt aged 15

I woke up at 6am to find our tent being battered by rain. Dad said we wouldn't move until the rain had ceased. It did cease for 30 minutes at one point but I was still asleep.

We finally packed the tent and set off at about 10am. On the way to Lussac I managed to fall off my bike during a descent, getting my front wheel stuck in a ditch and cutting my elbow, shoulder and knee. We also almost got mown down by a skidding ambulance.

Dad bought some cakes in Lussac, then some water in the next little town called Persac. In L'Isle-Jourdain we had lunch - rolls with ham and apricots. After that we took a long road to Abzac, which was a quiet town with red-tiled roofs, then onto Saint Germain where there was a bridge with a pretty view. Then we reached Confolens, although we only entered the outskirts of Confolens having decided the printed route was crap.

We turned off onto a 'D' road that took us up a huge hill, on top of which we had a widdle. Then, after many photos, we reached Lesterps, where Dad bought us some water and a soft drink. The second from last stop was Brigueil, where we bought ham, saucisson, peaches, wine and cheese.

We arrived at the campsite in Saint Junien at 6pm. We set up the tent then went for bread and water. After that we had a wash and cleaned our clothes and ate dinner: pâté from yesterday, saucisson, ham, bread, cheese, chocolate, peaches, cake and wine.

We went to phone Mum in the town centre before coming back and going to sleep.

We travelled 103.3km today.

After hopefully a good night's sleep, we want to go further than printed on the sheet tomorrow.

Arthur aged 42

Rained all night so I was not able to get my washing dry. Also raining in the morning, so we did not make a start until 10am, which was particularly late. It was, in fact, really only drizzle but because we were under a tree, every time the wind blew it seemed like it was raining harder. The sun came out when we started riding.

Missed by a skidding ambulance earlier in the day. Matt fell off, kerb crawling, but fortunately nothing serious.

Made good headway considering our late start. Got some nice almond tarts at Lussac, which we ate for tea. Took a diversion from the route at Confolens and came into town on a 'D' road instead of an 'N' road.

Good descents today, one for about two kilometres. Scenery is very different now. Lots of red roofs, and I find the old farms look like the set from The Three Musketeers. Nice area. Nearly past Limoges.

Highlights of the day.
— The lady in charge of the campsite wore a uniform.
— Excellent dinner with lots of choice.

Matt aged 36

With the heat really hampering us yesterday afternoon, last night we decided today would be an ultra-early set-off to make hay while the sun doesn't shine. So we wake at 6.15am. Good grief, that's early for me. With nobody stirring in any of the tents nearby the campsite is like an eerie scene from a horror movie.

My first job, as it has been for the last few days, is to try to clean and prepare my sore bits while dad is doing his ablutions. So out come the wet wipes, Healing Gel and cotton pads.

And as I'm rooting around down there I find a strange hanging nodule attached to my scrotum. (Please excuse the graphic nature of this.) Sweet Lord, has some part of me become distended? It's one thing being in pain, it's quite another to cause yourself lasting physical damage, especially round the undercarriage of all places. I try pulling this hideous dangleberry, but it's very tender. I feel a bit sick.

As soon as dad gets back from his ablutions I'm off to the loo, wondering what to do. First Legionnaires' disease, now this. Perhaps we should just give up? I decide to have another feel around in the privacy of a cubicle, and I realise this swinging globule moves a bit if you pull it gently. I keep pulling, despite the pain, and it comes away in my hands. Argh!

However, it's only a bit of congealed cotton wool that's been trapped by some pubes. Phew. Sort of.

So, back to what passes for full strength these days, I return to the tent and help pack up. We try to leave most of the ants behind. By 7.30am we're ready to roll — the campsite gates are open, the road awaits.

But to add to the physical discomfort, I'm knocked emotionally just a little. As we set off I see two little chaps in their pyjamas going to the shower block to brush their teeth. They must be about the same age as Ad and Davey, and I can feel the same itch under my nose and the water welling below my eyes as I felt the day we left home. The tears don't break the dam, but I'm missing the boys.

I take the lead on the road so that dad doesn't see I'm upset and we retrace our route a few hundred yards back to dad's favourite wine shop of yesterday evening.

Even though I'd gone through the start of today's journey on the map and in my head last night, I still have to revert to the phone to show us the exact way out of Chasseneuil. Then we're onto small 'D' roads, ignoring our official route again. First waypoint is Saint Julien l'Ars. Was Saint Julien a martyr? In which case he must have died on his Ars. I know the feeling. In the circumstances it's something of a shame it's not St Matthieu l'Ars.

Arthur aged 63

I had a rather poor night, no surprise given the proximity of the road and the TGV. In fact, I woke up just after midnight, then just before one o'clock, and again just before three o'clock. So by dawn's crack — around 06.15hrs — I decide to get up.

We decamp and set off at 07.30hrs. The sun is hiding behind the clouds, meaning it won't get too stressful just yet. We manage to set a good pace and breakfast beckons as we near Saint Julian l'Ars. We make for the cake shop and I purchase the mandatory pains au chocolat, two delicious fruit tarts and some Oranginas, which are becoming Matt's early morning energisers. What he does not drink he mixes with the water in his drinking bottle, which he finds is very nice.

A friendly Frenchman asks us where we are going, so I have a brief conversation with him. As we eat in the alcove beside the cake shop, the eighteen-wheelers chug past. I think we may have caught the 'rush hour', or whatever they call it in France.

After breakfast, dad is convinced he's seen a sign for a sports shop. He'd like to get a saddle cover for my saddle, which he is now using. I ask if it's hurting but he says it's fine. He does seem a trifle confused, though. There's no sports shop, and although he knows our next stop is a town called Tercé, he stands in front of a huge road sign with an arrow pointing right for Tercé, only to call back: "Straight on, yes?"

"No dad. Right. Just as that huge sign next to you says."

We leave the sanctuary of the boulangerie and head down the street. I forget where we are going, but I end up standing beneath the road sign and tell Matt it is in the opposite direction. We are headed for Tercé — that's the one — and set off again, in the right direction this time.

We reach the tiny village just before 09.00hrs. This is unquestionably an upmarket area because it has a public toilet which caters for both men and women.

Matt goes in search of water while I remove myself to a decent distance away from 'les sanitaires'. This puts me just across the road from the church and the inevitable war memorial, and arguably the only roundabout for miles around.

I do not see the actual impact but I certainly hear the sound of a calamity. I turn to look towards the roundabout again. A car, attempting to go around the island in the middle, has misjudged the distance and crashed into the kerbing on the far side. The front suspension has not coped well with this, and in consequence the right front wheel is now running at 90 degrees to the direction of travel. At moments like this you don't know where to look, but I do spot the passenger exiting the vehicle and try to kick the errant front wheel straight. A very noble gesture, given he is wearing flip-flops.

The car is going nowhere until a burly van driver arrives and assists in pushing it into the nearby church car park. I pretend to be taking photos of the war memorial, but manage to sneak a couple of the damaged car. After the collapsing exhaust episode in La Pouëze, I am beginning to think that car maintenance is something else the French do not worry about. I find this rather odd, given the hair-raising speeds at which they drive and how intimate they like to get with the rear bumper of the car in front.

I can't really be too cocky about car disasters. I, too, have had a long and not always distinguished history with motor vehicles. (Although in fairness to myself, most of my disasters have been the result of mechanical failings rather than bad driving.) There was the time my exhaust came off and I had to remove my jumper, tie one end to the passenger door handle and run the jumper under the car to the other side where I could hold up the exhaust while driving somewhere I could affect better repairs. Or the night I had to reverse home — miles, and in the dark — because I'd lost all forward gears. I wasn't stupid, of course, I reversed on the correct side of the road, except when I reached a 'No Entry' near home, where I reasoned with myself that at least the car was pointing in the right direction.

Or there was the time, in my efforts to make my Mini Cooper go faster, I fitted a Weber carburetor. I made what is called a 'cold air box' from an old paint tin and fibre-glassed this into the bulkhead of my Mini. It all worked well. However, one Saturday night as I drove through the lanes to Susan's house, the blasted thing back-fired and I saw flames coming out from the glass-fibre bonnet. It was rather worrying, but fortunately they disappeared as fast as they had arrived and I reached my destination unscathed.

Of course, all that happened when I was a young fellow. I'm marginally more sensible now.

As much as I would like to say that I have lived in LA, New York City, Berlin or even London, it has never happened and I have lived in Jersey in the Channel Islands all my life. I know this is not very cool but I'm managing to cope with it. To make it even worse, I have not just only lived in Jersey, I have also lived in the same parish for most of my life. But, as I say to people who I show around the island: "Why should I move, if I already live in paradise?"

Whether or not Jersey is paradise is a personal opinion.

Certainly I have seen a lot of changes in the island. In the 1950s, when I was born, the island had a population of around 55,000 people, rather than the 100,000 who live there now. The main industry was farming; potatoes, tomatoes and cattle were major exports. There were other jobs, of course. At that time my dad was a mason who built granite walls. In the years before the German Occupation of Jersey he had been a farmer, but he abandoned farming when the Germans arrived and took up a role as a tree feller. Because there was a lack of all kinds of fuel during the Occupation, he was kept very busy.

Strangely enough, today I live only about 500 yards from where I lived until I was 11 years old. I remember that there were acres of greenhouses nearby, and that the workers bought their supplies from the local store which I knew as Miss Le Meur's shop (it's now called Midland Stores). One Sunday, my mum and dad must have pushed the boat out because I remember going to call on Miss Le Meur at her back door to buy a block of ice-cream. In those days we had our ice-cream given to us tightly wrapped in layers of newspaper in an effort to stop it melting.

I don't think that I strayed far away from home. My first school was based in a big room on the nearby cattle farm. We had nature study walks around the area and did things like 'music and movement', which came to us via the radio. One of the best days during the school year was when the cattle show came to the field opposite the school. That afternoon we did no schoolwork but instead attended the show and enjoyed exotic treats like Smiths' crisps (that had a small bag of salt supplied inside) and lemonade. A bar was set up among straw bales in an outbuilding and, because it was 'licensed', we had to get an adult to buy us whatever we wanted.

It was at this point that I developed my interest in cycling. By the time I was seven or eight I eventually fitted the bicycle that my parents had bought me some time earlier and I would go off exploring the lanes that I knew well from my walks at school. In those days it was important that children grew into their clothes, shoes and bicycles. I remember buying that bike at Phil Duvey's shop, one of three bike shops that lined one particular street in Jersey's capital, Saint Helier. I also well remember that I could barely reach the pedals, so it took some time and several hundred laps of our front lawn before I felt confident to ride.

When I was 11 we moved to a bungalow that my dad built in Saint Martin. This was in the depths of the countryside by local standards, and from memory I cycled to and from my preparatory school, a round trip of about eight miles. This was a great place to grow up: the beach was just below us and the breakwater at Saint Catherine was only a short stroll away through a tomato field or two. I used to follow boyish pursuits like searching rock pools and fishing from the breakwater. I never caught anything. In fact if I had *thrown a stone with a £20 note wrapped around it into the sea it would have had the same result and saved me hours of wasted time.*

Back then Jersey itself appeared to be wholly focused on tourism. There were hundreds of hotels, guesthouses, pubs and tearooms. Almost every hotel had a cabaret and many of today's household names — not least the Chuckle Brothers — started here. It would not be unusual to see 20 or 30 tourist coaches on a drive around the island, and the beaches were packed with deckchairs and happy holidaymakers. Some of these visitors still return to the island every year, despite a massive decline in numbers starting around the 1970s.

Nowadays farming and tourism have not completely disappeared, but finance and the law are at the cornerstone of the island's economy. Our comfortable taxes and the simplicity that computerisation has brought to trading has projected Jersey into the world of corporate law and accountancy. So goodbye to Hedley Le Vesconte with a Bedford lorry and dirt under his fingernails, and hello to Jason Fforbes-Brown. Jason is something big in compliance, he runs an Audi and wears a Canali suit. Unlike Hedley, he has a credit card. I suppose many places in Britain, Europe and worldwide have gone through similar transformations, it's just the insular nature of living on a small island can make the changes seem starker. That said, I'm personally just as happy chatting to Jason as I am to Hedley.

This morning the weather is very definitely on our side. It's cool enough and the cloud cover looks pretty secure at the moment. The fields either side all seem a lot more verdant than yesterday's wide open expanses. That might be partly due to conditions overhead, but I think it's also a sign we're reaching a valley area with its richer soil.

The roads are smooth and quiet — perfect cycling conditions — so it's no surprise to meet a pack of old-boy roadies out on a training loop. They all happily shout hello. I always say, "Bonjour", but dad shouts out, "Salut". He says that makes him sound like he's from the south of France and therefore cooler. I think I'll stick with "Bonjour".

As the road emerges from between some trees I spot two towers spewing vapour in the distance. "Look dad, it's a cloud factory," I shout. It really does look like the cloud cover is emanating from there. In fact, it's the nuclear power station at Civaux on the banks of the Viennes, near to Planète des Crocodiles — an attraction that certainly caught my attention when I saw its name on the map. With the power station so close by it conjures up ideas of mutant killer lizards, but actually I think it's just a crocodile zoo. We'll be heading towards those towers and crossing the river nearby.

It takes a little while but soon we are descending through pretty hill-land farms, near an incredible fairy-tale-perfect castle at Morthemer, and then down to the Vienne riverbank. Sure enough there's the impressive power station. As much as dad and I would love to feel superior, we certainly can't talk about sympathetic placement of massive civic facilities. Jersey has a power station and incinerator slap-bang on an otherwise attractive coastline, and the UK is awash with similar abominations. A few years ago I did a feature ride from Portmeirion dressed as 'The Prisoner' from the eponymous cult 1960s TV series, and stumbled upon a decommissioned nuclear power station in pretty north-west Wales. So both the places I call 'home' have a poor track record.

The funny thing about Jersey and the UK is that I don't call both places home at the same time. When I'm in Jersey and I refer to home I mean the area south of Croydon just inside the M25 — that's where Manda, the boys and I live. But if I say to Manda, "I'll just call home," it means I'm ringing mum and dad in Jersey. It all makes perfect sense in my head.

What doesn't make perfect sense, at least to people in England, is why anybody would want to leave Jersey. They seem to have this strange notion that it's always sunny (it certainly isn't) and it's as glamourous as Bergerac made it look. I'm not quite sure what I mean by that statement — Bergerac and glamour is an oxymoron to my mind — but you sort of get what I mean. To many people Jersey is an island, it's a bit different, it's not like 'boring' England.

Wherever you come from rather frames your experience of life, and that's never more true than when you come from somewhere relatively unusual. Funnily enough, I'm one of a very rare breed: because all my parents and grandparents were born in Jersey — a non-EU territory — I used to be one of the less than 10 per cent of people who live in the island who aren't entitled to an EU passport. My passport always said EU on the front but when you turned to the back page there was a disclaimer that said: "The bearer of this passport has no rights to live or work in the European Union".

That issue about passports is a moot point for me now. I've lived in the UK for so long — the one EU territory where a Jersey person does have a right to live and work — that I'm now an EU citizen anyway. But with such family heritage in the island, moving away wasn't something that came naturally.

However, it was the best thing Manda and I could ever do. If you want to go to university and get a proper degree, you have to leave the island. And once I'd decided I wanted to be a journalist, and I had fairly big dreams, I realised there are only so many media outlets on an island nine miles long by five miles wide. Add to that all the opportunities to really experience life — to see shows, sports events, music concerts, national celebrations — and to be near where the news is really happening, and living on the 'the mainland' seemed preferable to being adrift in the Channel.

When we first starting making a life for ourselves in the UK, people back home would always say: "Aren't you scared living in England? Isn't it dangerous?" They seemed to think all the stories they read about in the *Daily Mail* or saw on the BBC news at six o'clock were happening on every street corner from Southampton to Stornoway. Conveniently, they'd also ignore Jersey's relatively high levels of drug abuse, alcoholism, town violence and suicide.

But seeing how much Manda and I continue to enjoy our lives in England, people in Jersey don't ask those questions any more. Places change, and so do people. I'm sure I've altered and my perception of Jersey has morphed a little. Wherever you were born and raised, if you've lived away for almost 20 years you're bound to feel slightly detached. But if anything, that means I'm softening towards the motherland a little. Had I written this 10 years ago, the book would almost certainly be banned from the island's shores. That said, other than missing my mum, dad and uncle, there's no reason why I'd want to live there.

Another thing about living away is that I can be my own person. In a relatively small community like an island, no matter what I did or achieved I would always be 'Arthur's son'. That's fine, I love dad and I'm very proud of him. But I'd prefer to be defined by who I am and my abilities, rather than somebody's potentially misguided idea of my family history.

In any case, my opinion is that Jersey nowadays is essentially like any other equivalent-sized British town. It's just that while British towns tend to be surrounded by motorways, Jersey is surrounded by water. That makes it a bit harder and more expensive to visit or escape. But with the island receiving the same British TV and radio, and with at least 40 per cent of Jersey residents being first generation immigrants from the UK, the prevalent culture — now — is essentially the same as anywhere else in the British Isles.

Obviously dad can't say that. His job as a tourist guide is to tell holidaymakers how great and special Jersey is. That's fine. What I can forgive less easily is his support for the French rugby team. Mum keeps reminding him his grandchildren are English, but he shouts "Allez les bleus" anyway.

We'll see if he's still such a fan by the time we reach Sète.

Now we're on a relatively big 'D' road making good speed to Lussac. It's only just 12 o'clock but we had such any early start it feels like it's well past lunchtime already. The sun is up high and bright again, so we aim for Lussac's centre ville and hope for some shelter. A friendly chap shouts hello from his shed as we pass. He seems to be making puppets. Suppose it beats doing bugger all like everybody else over here.

There are lots of cafés open in the pretty town centre but we can't find a sandwich shop. I do spot a small boulangerie with cakes, though, so I buy two large apple flan things. I ask the lady if there is anywhere else nearby that sells sandwiches. She says no. We eat our flans sitting on a doorstep trying to find some shade. A Frenchman walks past and coughs. Even his cough sounds French: full of phlegm.

I change the map on my handlebar bag — quite a protracted chore, involving clips, Velcro and cord — and we head off. Around the corner, not more than 50 yards from where that boulangerie woman told me there were no sandwich sellers, there's another boulangerie with a window filled with baguettes, and the baguettes themselves are filled. I'm tempted to think that the apple flan lady was a lying vache.

At this point we should be trying to get the miles in, but I spot a big supermarket as we leave Lussac and think it could be one of the few chances we'll have to buy dad's MicroSD card. Getting hold of this has become something of a personal challenge for me. I pop in and sure enough they have one. Well done Lussac, you are mid-France's portal to the 21st Century.

Sweet lord it's getting warm again and there's a strangely seaside-y feel to the white-washed houses as we leave the town. But soon we're in among trees, and because we've climbed a fair bit recently, we're swooping down and up the valleys of Vienne tributaries.

The road ahead promises quiet lanes running downhill alongside the Vienne, or at least that's how I remember it from last time. Yes, we ride beside the Vienne on quiet lanes, but it does not seem to be going downhill much. These little roads have the bits that need repairing marked with fluorescent paint, they do something similar back in Jersey (I wonder if they get repaired here?). I notice that my quadriceps are getting bigger and are squaring off at the front as well. This is a great appearance if you cycle, although hopefully I will not end up looking like I have two pillows strapped to my thighs, which is not such a great look.

We head for L'Isle-Jourdain, a stop dad remembers from last time as the venue for one of our 1994 photos. In a village called Persac we have a choice: continue on the D11, which isn't a terrible road; or turn left and follow the riverbank. We're supposed to be doing this ride for enjoyment — that's been slipping our minds recently — so we decide to go for the river route. Also, we reckon there's more chance of finding tree shade down there.

It is a good choice and proves to be a glorious route, following the deep blue Vienne up river as it twists and turns.

We enter the village of Moussac. I get my bearings and explain the directions to dad: first right, then first left. A lady walks past and asks if we're lost. "Ah non," the old chap says, and then perfectly explains the directions we'll be taking to her. Good, he's been listening.

We start pedalling again, take the first right, then he promptly sails past the next left. "Whoah, hold up there," I shout. "What happened to the first left?"

"Don't we have to cross the river first," he says.

"No. Why did you think that? You never said that to that woman just now?" I reply incredulously.

I think the heat is getting to us both.

Still, no need for stroppiness. This really is fine cycling territory and great for photos, too. I'm keen that we have a snap together, and there's a British car parked in the driveway of a house near a particularly picturesque spot. I can see somebody in the garden, so I go to ask if they'll take the shot. Somehow they disappear from view. I go back and tell dad.

"He must have been a bit of a funny fella," dad says, that universal 'funny' adjective getting an airing again.

We soon realise the luxury of having had a route largely shaded by trees. The road into L'Isle-Jourdain is open and we start to really feel the sun beating down on us. I also feel a little bit like we're back in England. Almost all the cars that pass us have UK number plates and a lot of the homes in more scenic areas have British cars parked outside. The French must hate us, although there's no sign of that as we pull into L'Isle-Jourdain and notice an English-French translation company.

It is very, very hot and sunny. We have a reprise at L'Isle-Jourdain, a place that I remember from our last trip. We pull up in the square. It's 14.30hrs so we decide to have a lunch break in the shade of some trees.

Matt goes in search of food and has an amazing stroke of luck. Although everything is shut from noon until 3pm — due to the heat no doubt — the lady at the Co-Op supermarket opens up for him and he buys a great spread again. While he's doing this, I listen to a family row going on through the open window just above me. I can't quite follow what the problem is, but a young lad emerges a few minutes later and exchanges pleasantries with me about cycling.

Because the nice lady in the Co-Op opens just for me — and even switches the lights on — I load my hand basket with grub to make her efforts worthwhile.

Fresh faced and ready to ride. Just about to board the ferry to Saint Malo in 1994.

Getting ready to board the ferry to Saint Malo in 2015, with significantly less hair.

The first drink and shelter stop, where Arthur was introduced to the wonders of the electrolyte tab.

Tomorrow morning's alarm clock.

Pizza time. At this point everything is going rather well.

The scene of Matt's close encounter with Legionnaires' disease.

Fun's a-coming – it's time to take a pill.

Asterix by the roadside.

Then and now...

...Crossing the Loire.

Outside the strange chapel after Chalonnes.

More worringly - inside the strange
chapel after Chalonnes.

No bacon or sausages for us this morning, despite the temptation.

An industrial edifice on the outskirts of Neuville.

Paying by the ant in Chasseneuil de Poitou.

Two flies having a far better time than we are. Pervy ant looks on.

The beautiful Vienne Valley.

Two clowns spoiling the view of the beautiful Vienne Valley.

Eat your heart out Friends of the Earth. Our photographic statement about Civaux's nuclear power station.

Looks like he's caught a bottle of Loic Raison cider. What are the chances?

The pretty weir at Chabanais.

A rare chance to be in the same photo together thanks to some visitors in Châlus.

Then and now...

...The phone box in Ladignac le Long.

Ségur le Château. A pretty place for breakfast, even in the rain. Idiot with cat just out of shot.

Despite the conditions, the old chap's morale never wavers. The person taking the pic isn't quite so cheery.

The hillside town of Turenne.

Then and now...

...Crossing the Dordogne.

At last, something to cheer him
up in Latronquière.

Matt uses Google Maps
to record where he's left
his lungs.

The wonderfully pretty town of Salles la Source.

The statue at the summit
of the Col d'Aujols.

Millau's imposing 1,000ft high viaduct.

Climbing out of Millau in the early morning.

The barren Causse du Larzac. It was either this or a dual carriageway.

Saint Pierre de la Fage. All we needed was an Ennio Morricone tune to complete the wild west atmosphere.

The view from the Col du Vent. Somewhere down there is the sea.

Then and now....

...Among the vines of southern France.

Our first sight of the sea since Saint Malo.

In Sète at last.

Two days later... back off the ferry and
with our best pals.

This includes some Hollywood chewing gum for Davey when we get back, and I find cider for dinner tonight.

Dad's been taking some pictures while I shop, then we sit to eat under a tree in the town square. Everything is closed but at least the sun's working hard. One of my knees is slightly out of the shade and I can actually feel the skin on it sizzling. I've been applying sunspray fairly regularly all trip, but even factor 30 has barely been able to put up a fight over the last couple of days.

From L'Isle-Jourdain it's only 20 miles or so on a big 'D' road to our planned stop today at Confolens. In normal conditions we'd be able to rattle that off in a couple of hours, but I worry about any kind of mileage after 1pm.

That fear is well founded. After taking 10 minutes or so to get myself settled on the saddle — I've adopted a slightly skewiff position to try to protect the crevice on the left side of my groin — we're pedalling hard, but it's so hot that we have to stop every four miles or so to seek shelter for a little while.

Strangely, we're both incredibly full of wind. Dad is burping like a human frog, and I'm sneaking — or not so sneaking — it out in other ways. We have a discussion while we rest under the trees about which is the most offensive. I'm tempted to go with burping as it's so overt.

I turn on my phone map app just to check where we are and set off again. The next stop we face is unplanned, as there are roadworks with traffic lights and the carriageway has become a one-way single lane. That's fine, until we realise it goes on for more than a mile and it's uphill. I really can't pedal much more, so we hop off and push. Then one of the roadworks cars drives up behind us, lights flashing like an emergency vehicle. Effectively it's our very own state-funded French broomwagon. The driver isn't impatient but it's obvious nothing can come the other way until we've cleared this section. We hop on again and ride as best we can. Eventually we're free.

After lunch, back on the bikes, we have to take constant breaks. I abandon my cycling mitts and bike helmet, opting instead to wear a cloth engineer's cap. Matt says it has a certain Karl Pilkington Idiot Abroad look to it, which may suit me. In any case, it gradually takes on a faux camouflage appearance as time goes on and as I perspire more and more.

Eventually we cross a huge 'D' road on top of a hill, then descend to Saint Germain de Confolens. Dad is under the impression that we're at our destination, but I'm afraid he's a bit premature. It's very pretty and olde worlde but the campsite we want is actually found outside the town that's known just as 'Confolens', a couple of miles away. The route here is very enjoyable, though: smooth, sheltered under trees and largely flat. I tell dad our campsite today is called Camping des Ribières and it's right on the banks of the river, so it should be easy to find. Proving that craziness comes in threes, for the third time today he seems determined to go off-route, and looks primed to dart up a side road, following a sign labelled quite clearly as a view point.

We decide to stay at Confolens, which we hope promises a campsite by the river. We are not disappointed. Camping des Ribières is undoubtedly the best site that we have visited so far. The staff are very friendly, there are few other people about, and we can choose any pitch that we want. Naturally we camp right beside the river. I tie our bottle of cider to the washing line and lower it into the water to cool.

After yesterday's farrago, today's campsite is heaven. It is modern with a fridge full of cold drinks and a chest freezer full of ice-creams. The site is green, clean and all but empty so we can have our pick of the pitches. There's even free Wifi. We sign in and choose a spot right next to the river.

Before I can say, "But you can't swim", the old chap is down the bank with the cider and his hi-tech washing line in hand, and he's dangling the bottle in the river to make it cool. I point out that for a man who freaks out at an ant or two in his food, he seems rather laissez faire when it comes to whatever bugs or bacteria are in that water. He replies that we're not going to lick the bottle, we're just going to drink what's inside it.

It's a quiet campsite. There are some English people in a campervan occupying the pitch to our left, and there's a French couple who are on a cycle tour to the other side. Nearby, there's also a miserable couple of young male and female French road cyclists who don't seem to be chatting to each other. She's just come back from a ride out alone and now they're sitting there in silence, eating dinner on their poxy camping table. I don't know why, but communal camping sights like these two — obviously miserable in each other's company — are really starting to annoy me. Perhaps it's because I'm missing Manda.

We set up the tent (discovering a few insect stowaways from this morning), get ourselves sorted and I go for a shower. There are no nests of creepy crawlies today, so even after a painful arse-fixing procedure morale is high. Dad pops to the campsite office and buys extra water and some cans of fizzy drinks. Then, when he goes for a shower I go out and buy some more drinks — my opinion is that we can never have enough — as well as some cola and lemon flavour Calippo shots in memory of the boys. We have a good dinner of bread, cheese, cider and biscuits.

What a great site, very quiet and scenic, and not expensive. Perhaps the only downside of the place is the lack of toilet seats. You either have to have a very wide bum or a fantastic sense of balance.

From our tent we have a superb view of the river just in front of us, with a watermill standing about 300 yards away on the far bank. In addition to this, we are entertained by the antics of a few brave souls who have decided to hire a rowing boat and make their way upstream.

This is more like it. If we can have a few more campsites like this, it'll make the days in the saddle seem a little more worthwhile.

After a call home we get ready for bed and I prepare the route for tomorrow. In theory it's a short day— something like 50 miles — so if we get an early start we should be able to reach Saint Yrieix la Perche, our goal, in good time.

There are more church bells going off. It sounds like a war has started. To be honest, it may take nothing short of a war to get me to leave this place tomorrow morning.

DAY 6
Like A Horse And Carriage

Friday August 19, 1994 — Saint Junien to Lubersac (57.7 miles)
Friday August 7, 2015 — Confolens to Saint Yrieix la Perche (56.8 miles)

Matt aged 15

Dad woke early but I didn't get up until 7.15am. We packed our stuff fairly quickly and left at 8am. We first encountered a large hill then a long descent into Rochechouart. Unfortunately, we missed one of our turnings and so had to follow the 'D' road all the way down.

After Rochechouart we climbed a steep hill and went to Cradour, where Dad bought us two biggish cakes and five chocolate croissants. We ate these and then went on our way to Châlus. Then, after a lot of hills through forests, we arrived at Ladignac where we had a peach and some cakes. I broke three spokes. Dad had to fix them.

We went on to Saint Yrieix la Perche where we bought food for tea:, duck pâté, two baguettes, white wine and fishy cakes. In Saint Yrieix a woman running the boulangerie thought Dad was French! We bought more spokes in Saint Yrieix. We also saw loads of Luc Leblanc signs written on the road and what we thought was a hill prime line from the Tour de France. Getting out of Saint Yrieix was a problem as it was steep and complicated.

We continued to Ségur le Château, which was a really old town, and then to our destination at Lubersac. Finding the camp here proved tricky.

We set up the tent, had a shower, did the washing and Dad fixed my bike. We had white wine, cakes, baguettes, ham, cheese and the fishcakes for tea. Then we went to phone Mum.

In total we travelled 92.9km today but went very slowly in the afternoon due to boiling weather. All day I suffered with a really sore bum. Dad broke his computer.

Tomorrow, after hopefully a good night's sleep we will go well.

Arthur aged 42

Earlier start than yesterday. A good climb out as usual. Missed a turning and went onto Châlus, with not a great deal more mileage.

Made good progress until lunch when Matt broke three spokes on a pavement. Had to remove bags, wheel, tyre and tube to fit the spokes we carried. Bought 10 more spokes in Saint Yrieix. Also bought tea there and a phone card.

Dropped my computer and it lost the last two digits. Last few kilometres were hard as usual, with a lot of walking up hills. Did a bit extra on the suggested mileage today to finish in Lubersac.

Matt is cycling better. We raised saddle slightly and he is spinning the gear rather than struggling. Saint Yrieix is big Luc Leblanc country. Signs on the road on the way there. Apparently he married a local girl.

Highlights of the day:

— We saw a Tour de France climb finish line across the road.

Matt aged 36

Early kick-off again today. In fact, it's very dark as we get up. I go through the same old process as always: wake, teeth, address the first 'burning issue' of the day, pack bags, take down tent, then scarper.

The roads are fairly quiet as we cross a little bridge towards Confolens. Then we simply follow the Vienne upstream, keeping the river to our right as we head for the first town of the day: Chabanais. Last night, as I planned our route, I had a tricky choice to make. The official directions would have us going on a big 'D' road to Saint Junien, but we know the route by the river is pretty and the roads are safe, so I've opted for this instead.

The problem is, apart from little triangles denoting steep road sections and a few spot heights, these Michelin maps give no hint of general gradients. So I don't really have any idea about what conditions we'll face in terms of climbing. The sun's already out by about 8am. For all the good points of this route, it's very wibbly-wobbly and far from direct. The way I'm feeling, I just want to get where we're going as quickly as possible.

At least today should be a short day. Had we reached Saint Junien last night we'd only be looking at 42 miles. As it is, we shouldn't have much more than 50 miles in the saddle to reach Saint Yrieix. So hopefully we'll get back on track and arrive there early.

Arthur aged 63

I think that by now I must be hydrating sufficiently because I had to get up in the night to visit the facilities — it's one of the signs of becoming officially 'an old man'. After a very quiet night otherwise, I'm up at 06.00hrs. I can't hear any cars rushing by in the distance, maybe we are too early even for them at this hour? By 07.00hrs we have taken the tent down and done all the typical 'breaking camp' stuff. As usual, it is almost impossible to dry the inside of the tent, despite using our super-small, super-absorbent travelling towels.

Packed and ready to go, we hop aboard the bikes and roll along the irregular tarmac that makes up French roads. Soon we are once again in the groove, metaphorically speaking. Our route runs beside the Vienne, an old friend from the last odyssey. Like us, the river is heading for the sea, but unlike us it is going at its own leisurely pace. A pace that is much slower than even we manage on bicycles, and it doesn't have to go up hills.

We accompany the Vienne for some distance, leaving it as we search for quiet roads and then meeting it again briefly before climbing for what seems like forever just after Chirac. It seems like this is the longest hill in the world (although I think that might actually be coming in the days ahead) and the audience of black and white heifers that look on over the hedge do nothing to make us feel any better. I imagine that they are confused to see humans struggling past like beasts of burden, puffing hard and wobbling about on metal things with wheels. Thankfully, we make it to the top and are able to freewheel most of the way into Chabanais. We stop for breakfast and a telephone call home. The view of the bridge and the river at Chabanais is excellent, however, the news from home about my GPS is not so good.

Chabanais appears and it's a pretty town. We come to a halt in a public car park in front of a busy little boulangerie and next to the scenic weir. Sunspray has to go on as I'm burning already. It's my left, eastward-facing leg that is taking the brunt of it. While dad gets his camera out I pop over the road to buy our breakfast.

The French people we've met so far tend to range from the supremely charming and pleasant to the thoroughly officious. The bustling little lady behind the till is a rare example of somebody who bridges the gap, quickly going about picking out various baguettes from the range behind her. Indeed, anyone who thinks a baguette is simply a 'French stick' would be educated here — there are at least 12 different types and sizes of very similar looking bread. I opt not to be flash and order a standard baguette, two pains au chocolat, two apple flan things and some drinks.

With people stacking up behind me in the shop, I pay and as I turn, I bump into an old crone who is seriously encroaching my personal space. My drinks crash to the floor. There's no way she or any of the other elderly clientele is bending down to help. (I can't help wondering what people of working age do over here — where are they all?) So I have to bend over excruciatingly slowly to retrieve the lost beverages. There's still no good news from 'down south' today.

Dad puts away his camera but then technology comes back to bite us. He wants to put the MicroSD card we bought yesterday into his GPS to expand its memory and be able to record the rest of our journey. He's down to having only two per cent of internal memory left (I'm talking about the GPS device here, not the old fella himself. Although...). We open the back of the machine and fit the new memory card, but it still reads 98 per cent full. There's no obvious way to sort this, so we phone home and mum has to go hunting for the manual.

When she rings back I take the call and listen to the instructions. It may be dad's machine but his relationship with technology is one of unrequited love. I will never forget the time I was watching him on the computer as he closed a document and the following warning appeared. "Do you want to save? If you don't, your work may be lost." Dad clicked 'No'.

I said to him: "But didn't you want to save that?"

"Yes," he replied.

"But you just clicked 'No'"

"Yes, it said my work might be lost. I don't want that so I clicked, 'No'," he replied.

When it comes to his GPS we could click anything we like, it will make no difference. Apparently, to get the SD card to work we need to plug it into a laptop computer. And that's one thing we haven't brought on this trip. Dad briefly considers the idea of buying one, but considering we're running out of power for our phones — he left his on last night — and other bits of kit, I don't think that's a viable option. In any case, c'est la France. Good luck finding a shop that both sells laptops and is open for business.

We've still got my phone and a borrowed Garmin Edge tracking our route, so we should be OK. But all this faffing around has lost us an hour already.

In truth, I'm a bit on edge today as it is. Last night was a great campsite and I wasn't keen to leave. More importantly, today is my wedding anniversary. Manda and I have been married 11 years. We've been together 18 years — half our lives. This is the first time we've been apart on our anniversary.

I met Manda in Jersey three months before we left for university. She is, and remains, the only woman I've ever actively and soberly pursued. That sounds a bit like I stalked her or something. What I mean is, I either fell into the very few other relationships I've had, or I was chatted up by the girl in question. That's more a testament to my reticence rather than lady-killer looks.

In the year leading up to me going to university, my mum — who is a pretty forward-thinking gal — said: "You'll meet all sorts of people when you're away. Don't get yourself lumbered with a Jersey girl before you go." It wasn't quite the: "Don't get anyone pregnant" speech, more: "Don't get anyone pregnant, at least not until you reach England." As for getting anyone pregnant, chance would have been a fine thing.

However, two truisms reared their head. The first is that hormone-driven 18-year-old boys tend to take the opposite of their parents' advice. The second is that mums are always right.

So I met Manda only a few months before we left Jersey, and while Manda was heading off to study in Brighton, I was going to university in Sheffield. It wasn't a good start. Add to that the immaturity of a young man among a smorgasbord of other young people, and our relationship during that first year at university was very much an on-off affair. I regret some aspects about my behaviour during that period, but not the overall experience; I think everybody should spread their wings and see what the world has to offer while they're young enough to get away with it.

In my case, I noticed a couple of things. The first was that most of the other women I was meeting shared a common trait — to a greater or lesser extent they were insane. I also noticed I was missing Manda, writing to her, thinking about her, even drawing pictures of her. It took that experience of being apart to understand we were soul mates.

The following summer holiday in Jersey we got back together, although I kept it secret from my folks for a little while. To mum and dad's credit, this was the only time they have ever given me any kind of talking to about my personal life and said I must not hurt Manda again. I didn't. Almost every weekend for the next three years, either Manda or I were on a National Express coach travelling between Sheffield and Brighton and having great fun (I use the word 'fun' both literally and euphemistically).

Right now, in Chabanais, I dream of any kind of fun. I'd even take National Express coach travel. In fact, any kind of travel would do.

Dad and I finally get our act in gear and we're climbing, yet again, out of the town.

I've noticed over the last few days that I'm rapidly falling in love with clouds and trees — they both stop the sun — and we're treated to a smattering of both. I'm also realising I hate downhills, as they undo all our good work so far. I want to hold onto every single foot of elevation gain that I can.

The 'D' road we have to take is relatively interesting, with twists and turns, although it seems to go up a fair bit more than it goes down. In many ways, this is about the closest I've come to imagining I'm on a road back home. We stop in the next village, Chassenon, for a drink and watch a portly roadie spin by. They have MAMILS — 'Middle-Aged Men In Lycra' — in France, too.

The next waymark is Rochecouart, which seems a packed little place, relatively speaking (c'est la France), although that might be because the roads are so small. Because the sun is massively hot again, I go searching for something to cool us down. There's a very smart boulangerie just down the road and it has an ice-cream chest. I try to open the freezer but it's locked.

The madame behind the counter looks over the queue she's serving and shouts something to me. I haven't got a clue what she's saying, but she's holding up a key, so I get the idea. Others in queue laugh, even the ones I've just seen getting out of a UK-registered car — filthy traitors. Still, there's the old French paranoia for you: quick Edith, lock the ice-cream cabinet!

In Rochecouart, Matt buys me some water and a Magnum, which threatens to lose its chocolate coating at the first opportunity.

We park on the pavement, which is rather narrow. In fact, it is so narrow that we are forced to constantly side-step into the road to let pedestrians pass. At moments like this, I wonder what the everyday French person thinks of us. Not much, I suspect. We arrive on bikes that look like mobile washing lines, we wear comfortable cycling clothes that flap about, and we are badly in need of a shave. This shabby look is miles away from the local coureurs we see, whose Lycra fits them like a second skin and whose legs glow with several applications of warming oil. Also these gods of the local cycling scene are super-clean shaven with legs to match.

This is probably a good time to explain why cyclists who aspire to look like professionals shave their legs. It is not because they are female impersonators in their spare time. Well, not usually. The smooth leg look serves two purposes. Firstly, it makes it easier to massage lactic acid out of tired leg muscles. And secondly, it lets you thoroughly clean the wounds that serious cyclists will inevitably suffer should they fall off. Most self-respecting riders would come up with that second reason, as it sounds much more macho. Very few mention, or maybe they don't know, that shaved legs cause less drag when you are looking for those elusive seconds in a time trial against the clock. I used to shave mine when I raced bikes — one of just many strange habits and hobbies my wife Susan has had to put up with over the years.

I have never thought of myself as particularly bright, but I do know what is good for me and being married is. If I had not fallen in love with Susan Knight, I would probably be clutching a can of Special Brew with all the other drunks in the park. Or worse yet, be in my grave, pushing daisies. I don't want to make too much of a big deal about this, but it is true.

By now it might be obvious that I am quite old-fashioned, but I am not as old-fashioned as Susan was. She flatly refused to live with me unless we were married. As we were both children of the swinging '60s this came as a surprise, but only the first of many that have come my way over the past 40 years.

It was a very measured courtship. In those days marriage was the usual route you took if you hoped to live together and have children, and we both felt that this was the right thing to do. It is probably fair to say the experience of those early days was definitely a primer for married life, especially for Susan. From memory, one of the less embarrassing things that came to pass included me trying to use half a lemon as an alternative to aftershave, only to end up in a sticky mess.

Most of my reminiscences from that time are car based. Susan and I used to spend a lot of time just driving round and, from time to time, the car might have a problem. One night, on the way to a romantic dinner I had to fix a loose battery connection, which wasn't a big deal until we realised I was covered in oil. Maybe not the best look with a suit.

But probably the luckiest escape Susan had involved an elderly ex-Post Office Morris Minor van, which I had bought from a bloke I knew who was a car mechanic. This van had seen better days, but nonetheless I did my best to get it in some kind of shape to convey my true love around. I knew it was going to be problematic as the previous owner had carried all sorts of dirty old car components in it. So I duly scrubbed the interior of the van including the floorpan, and — finding a tin of a rather attractive maroon gloss — I painted the inside of the cargo bay with it. I bought a sizeable area of foam matting and topped this off with a quality piece of paisley-patterned carpet that I got from a carpet fitter.

Perhaps unsurprisingly, this did little to impress Susan, who immediately noticed the huge holes in the floor — not quite big enough to put your foot through, but big enough to give you an unsurpassed view of the tarmac as we drove along. I used this van as my everyday transport for several weeks, until one evening as I returned home from work, it decided to collapse at a junction in the middle of town. A week or so later I sold the van to a mate for half price: £7.50.

Before marrying, as tradition and my buddies demanded, I was duty bound to have a hectic stag night (or what the French call 'the death of your life as a young man', which sounds rather dramatic and also quite final). I remember that Susan and her mum made trays of sandwiches for this event, although quite a few sandwiches were applied to the protagonists during the inevitable high jinks. This free-for-all took place at the premises of the Jersey Motorcycle and Light Car Club, where I used to spend a lot of my time. I was the club's publicity officer, so consequently I was quite popular and my request that I have my stag night there was readily agreed to.

I admit that almost 40 years later my memory has lapsed somewhat, and of course I was very drunk at the time. But I do remember soda water bottles being used to cool things down, and I particularly remember hooking the spout of a soda water bottle in the waistband of a buddy's trousers and giving him a good blast.

Understandably, I was not at the top of my game the next day, and my very understanding boss sent me home to recover. He said that he was surprised I even showed up at work at all. As usual I met Susan in the lunch hour and in an effort to make a speedy recovery, I bought a nice piece of steak and a bottle of Mattheus Rosé to wash it down. Have I said I was very fond of a drink in those days?

Despite all these excesses, I did make it to the church, looking very much the part in my penguin suit. I was happy to wear top hat and tails, after all it was only for a short time, but in some quarters it caused problems. My first choice of *best man and my dad refused to wear them, so I got another best man and my dad came in a suit with one of those über wide ties that were in fashion in the mid-'70s. The idea of going between the church and the reception in my Lotus Seven racing car was shelved, though. Rather a shame, but sense has to prevail from time to time. I do know someone who actually went on honeymoon in a very similar car, but probably not on open pipes and with a tiny two-gallon petrol tank.*

We survived the reception. My completely unprepared speech was interrupted on numerous occasions by my dad — no surprise there — but I managed to get to a conclusion. I often wonder why I had to endure this because, as requested, we had invited what my dad called "all my friends", most of whom he knew rather better than I did. Because of things like this, and the many other occasions where we had to go along with our parents' wishes, Susan and I try not to interfere with our sons' lives.

After almost 40 years, I suppose I should be able to give a reasonable idea of marriage to other people. Personally, I think that I've been extremely lucky. Not only is Susan completely undemanding and easy going, but also she is always 100 per cent behind my serial hobbies, ongoing paranoia and madcap ideas. Such as cycling across France again.

We head through the tight old cobbled streets out of Rochecouart but I quickly bring us to a halt. I've noticed a little back-alley computer shop, of all things, so I venture in to see if they have a USB lead that might connect dad's GPS to my phone (I'm hoping I can use my phone as external data storage and free up the GPS's internal memory). I'm met with a really nice, smiley lady who puts up with my bad French and helps me in English. She goes off to look for a lead but comes back empty handed. No matter, her cheery assistance has restored my faith in people after the bossy boulangeress.

The difficult terrain doesn't let up, though. We're not talking massive climbs, just a route that never really lets you take a breath. The big 'D' road snakes its way southwards among strangely manicured scenery. The farms look well defined, the hedges are kept back. Apart from the rolling terrain and my 'injuries', it's quite a pleasant, civilised experience. It does go on for a long time, though.

Over the course of the morning there's been a marked rise in the number of massive trucks coming past, and by the time we reach Oradour, the situation isn't funny. In among the twisty streets these big rigs seem lethally intimidating, so we try to get ourselves well out of the way. It's not all bad news. I've seen a sign for Saint Mathieu, although I have absolutely no intention of going out of my way to pay my namesake a visit.

Oradour has the obligatory pharmacy — the French must really go in for ailments in a big way, they're second only to churches in their ubiquity — but precious few other retail outlets. Round the corner I spot a tabac, so I head in to buy drinks while the old chap has a breather. The woman behind the counter doesn't input a cost in the till but charges me seven euros for two cans of Oasis and two bottles of water. I suspect she made up the frankly extortionate price in her head. Or perhaps I'm just catching the French paranoia bug. I wonder if the pharmacy has any treatment for it?

As we head out of Oradour dad spots a sign for a 'voie verte' — an off-road cycle path. I fight with the map to see where it heads. Praise be, it goes to Châlus, our next destination. That means we can relax a little bit and get away from the HGVs. We follow the signs, past the deathly quiet Office de Tourisme and Médiathèque, to find an old railway line that's been converted into a cycle route. This is a double whammy: not only will it be traffic-free but it should be flat, too.

It is lunchtime when we arrive in Orador sur Vayres and consequently it is like a ghost town. But on the plus side, we do find a voie verte. I have cycled on voie verte before, during my trip to Mont Saint Michel for the magazine article I wrote with Matt some years back. There, they were lovely and scenic, but not covered in tarmac like this one is.

At the start of the track here, an old station has been converted into toilets, so I stop to use the facilities. The light within is motion sensitive, but it goes out before I finish. Imagine my surprise when it comes back on as I shake the drips off.

Flushed with pride, I return to my bike and we proceed along the super smooth cycle track.

It is delightful, effortless cycling with trees on both sides and above us. Today we also seem to have it largely to ourselves. In fact, I've been very surprised throughout this entire journey to see very few French leisure or commuter cyclists. The majority of French riders appear to be old chaps clad in cycle racing kit, riding racing bikes of various vintages. So far, there has been no stereotypical everyday French folk, wearing berets and smoking Gauloises, aboard utility bikes laden down with their shopping.

Although mainly empty, on this track we do pass a group of cyclists who are on a motley collection of bikes. We offer the customary 'bonjours'. It is only when we stop and they overtake us that we realise they are not chatting to each other in French but in English.

The group disperses before we reach Châlus, but we catch up with some of them at the old Châlus Railway Station, which is used as a Tourist Office (it's shut at the moment. As Matt would say, c'est la France). We chat to our fellow Anglophones and find out they have a second home in the area. What could have been an exceptionally hilly day is turning out to be flatter, prettier and — having somebody else we can speak to in English — a little more interesting, too.

After what seems to have been a constant struggle since we got off the boat almost a week ago, the voie verte is truly care-free cycling. I'm from the video game generation, and it reminds me of a pipe in Marioland. You disappear down it and emerge, almost effortlessly, further along your route. OK, it's not quite effortlessly, but by our standards it's pretty close. By 12 o'clock the sky is overcast and the way is largely smooth, save for tree roots pushing up the concrete.

At the end of the trail, on the outskirts of Châlus, we overtake one family of riders and our fumble past each other reveals we have a shared native tongue. We start chatting and discover they're from Zimbabwe originally, then South Africa and have lived just outside Oxford for the last 20 years. They're interested in what we're doing and the chance to speak to somebody other than me has the old chap in full flow. I don't know if their eyes glaze over when he starts his Jersey tourist guide monologue about the history of the island, but I think mine probably do. That said, I'm piqued back into action soon.

"I used to run a bike shop," I hear dad say.

"Oh, what do you do now then?" they ask.

"Oh, I'm a tourist guide and a writer..." he says, "So's he," he continues, offhandedly tilting his head to me.

Now, please bear in mind I am very tired and emotional. But being referred to like this rather rubs me up the wrong way.

"Actually, I'm not a tourist guide," I interject. "I'm the editor of *What Cycle?* magazine and a journalist in the UK." I'm trying not to let my irritation show but I know I surely fail. I could go on about what I'm really thinking (I'm double IPC writer of year, chief writer of this, launch editor of that, author of those, blah blah blah) but it would sound pathetic. Essentially I felt that offhanded description was a slight disservice to my, albeit limited achievements, and I get the hump.

We keep chatting to the family and then I ask if they'd mind taking a picture of dad and me together. We have only a couple of joint photos from 1994 and none yet from this trip, so it would be good to get one in the bag.

We pose, the picture is shot, and we bid farewell. Then it's off to the nearby supermarket to buy lunch.

It's a fine place to get grub and I emerge with a veritable feast, including a two-litre plastic bottle of cider for tonight. Dad and I find a picnic table nearby and eat. It's a quiet lunch. I can't tell if dad's stroppy because I got the sweats up and embarrassed him, or if he's annoyed that he annoyed me. I'm annoyed that I'm still feeling slightly annoyed by it even now.

Pride can be a pretty dangerous emotion and one all men should try to keep in check. As I've mentioned, when Manda and I first moved to London, unable to get a break in journalism, I cleaned rental cars and vans for a year. I'm not too proud to clean vans again before I retire.

Funnily enough, though, it was pride that determined my resolution that Manda wouldn't marry me as a car cleaner. It was only after I joined *Cycling Weekly* as a sub-editor — what we might laughingly call a 'real' job — that I felt worthy enough to finally propose.

I asked Manda to marry me on July 4th 2003 at the Guilfest musical festival. Arthur Brown, The Darkness, The Wildhearts and Alice Cooper were all on the bill — it was a great gig. I had the ring in the top chest pocket of my leather jacket and I was so scared about losing it that I kept the jacket on all day. It was only once we got back to the car after the show that I finally had the courage to pop the question. I didn't get down on one knee, I hadn't asked her dad — I don't believe in all that nonsense — I simply asked my best friend if she'd like to get married. Thank God she said yes.

Our wedding day was the best day of my life. One of the reasons I enjoyed it so much was because it was one of the few times everybody was genuinely nice to me. Like most men, I spend a lot of my life being ribbed by family, children, friends, random strangers — that's fine, I can take it. You have to make sure those who love and respect you are also comfortable enough to take the mickey out of you. The old chap is a perfect example. We all mock him regularly but he takes it with incredible patience and good grace. I've seen families and companies ruled over by individuals who are almost cultishly revered. It's not healthy; no-one's perfect. If you can mix absolute affection with slight irreverence, I don't think that's so bad.

As usual, Matt comes out of the local supermarché with his arms full. We dine at a nearby stone table and benches, and watch the local refuse men emptying the rubbish bins as we eat.

Fortified with delicious vac-wrapped sandwiches that contained unusual fillings — you certainly can't fault the French sandwich maker's imagination — we cycle off towards our scheduled overnight stop at Saint Yrieix la Perche. It's a case of full steam ahead until I recognise a place from the last trip. We're keen to recapture as many images as possible from 21 years ago, so when I see the phonebox and the Chocolat Menier sign, the memories of fitting three spokes come flooding back. We set up the picture as best we can remember it and I snap away. Apart from my bike and a Mark III Ford Escort that was in shot back then, nothing at all has changed. This little village is actually called Ladignac le Long, something that I had not bothered knowing back in 1994.

Our climb out of Châlus to Bussière-Galant is truly awful and the sun is back out. Thankfully, there's then a great weaving route, almost Alpine in appearance and a lot of it downhill between wide green fields. The descents nearly give you enough impetus to get up each climb with gusto as they swerve round the terrain. It's quite a fun bit of road and in Ladignac dad spots the place where we took a photo back in 1994. Very little has changed. Let's face it, the whole country hasn't really changed much. We stop and try to recreate the shot.

As we carry on I see a heart-warming sight. There's a poster promoting the 48th Tour du Limousin bike race featuring some children in cycling gear. At the same time, a little chap probably aged 12 or 13 cycles towards us on his road bike wearing his club cycling jersey. I smile and say bonjour to this junior roadie, and I can't help thinking about my two boys wearing their Islabikes and Continental children's cycling kit. There's something magical about children and bikes.

Dad and I are now in the home stretch, on the way to our goal for the day at Saint Yrieix. Soon after Ladignac — with the map promising some up-arrow climbs to come — I decide to take us off the big 'D' road. Instantly we're leisurely pottering between farms and woodland. But so far every day on this trip has had a sting in the tail, and today is no different. First, the big bottle of cider that I thought had been securely held in place on my rack abandons ship. Then we hit a real soul-sapping little climb before descending into Saint Yrieix.

Saint Yrieix brings back memories of buying spokes at a friendly bike shop, talking about pro rider Luc Leblanc, and purchasing fish pastries from a woman in a cake shop. However, our ride towards it is marred marginally when the plastic bottle of cider that is elasticated to Matt's rear carrier makes a bid for freedom. It shoots across the road, leaving an exhaust trail of foam behind it, until it comes to a stop in a roadside ditch. I am behind and I pull up as fast as I can beside the rapidly diminishing cider. The screw top has broken as it bounced along the road and cider is now gushing out into the undergrowth. I pick it up and manage to pour about half the contents into my drinking bottle.

We are close to Saint Yrieix but one final climb stands in our way. It is at points like this that you get very stoic and just soldier on.

As we ride downhill towards the town centre I see a field to one side with what looks like pitches, a campervan and a few tents. Surely that's not the municipal campsite? It looks awful. Yet, when we reach Saint Yrieix we see signs for the municipal site pointing back the way we have just come. I seriously don't fancy that — there must be another campsite nearby.

We text home on our rapidly depleting phones but it takes ages for mum or Manda to respond. Just to confuse matters further, it seems the campsite here has changed names a bit in recent years. Rather than sitting on our bums, I suggest we go for a ride into centre ville. We try to follow signs for a supermarket that's supposed to be two minutes away, but it takes us uphill, far further than a two-minute drive, so we give up.

Instead, we stop at a boulangerie on the outskirts of Saint Yrieix, where I buy some cakes for dinner. Rather than paying the plump-faced woman behind the counter, I have to put my money into a special machine. I suppose it ensures the woman's hands stay clean for handling cakes. And for stuffing her face.

Eventually we decide we have no option but to follow the signs back to the campsite we passed. Except the signs don't take us to the campsite we passed: they veer off in a different direction. Unfortunately, the signs we're now following weren't visible in the direction we were originally coming from. Had they been, we could have arrived at this — the real campsite, hidden behind trees on the banks of a small lake — about an hour ago. C'est la France.

The welcome at a very modern and large reception centre is warm and professional, although the girl who takes my money is surprised when I say that we have arrived by bike. We are escorted to our pitch. Admittedly the campsite focuses on caravans and camping cars, but we have another great 'vue du lac' and a pitch so big that we could put four tents up in it. The showers and toilets are quite a distance away but worth the trip, providing you do not forget anything.

For some reason, dad asks not to be near the showers, which means we've got to walk up three or four terraces to the shower block. It reminds me of an army camp from my cadet days. Like most of the other campsites we've been to so far, there's a strange enforced bonhomie. And, as with army camp, there's a required greeting you have to make. Instead of saluting each person who passes, you have to smile and say "bonjour". Like crazed NCOs, some of the holidaymakers stare at you, almost daring you to disrespect them. I'm thoroughly unimpressed by it all.

It's been an odd day. We could have been here possibly two hours earlier had we not lost time in Chabanais with the GPS and then faffing about trying to find the campsite once here. The lost cider was a kick in the nuts, too. And I'm missing Manda and the boys. I'm starting to feel it all get to me.

After getting the tent up I walk towards the shower block. If I wasn't dispirited enough there's the repeated view of couples sitting in silence, eating their dinner while occasionally throwing the other a loaded glance over their fold-out table. Why are they so keen to get in my face to say bonjour but not speak to each other over dinner? Just chat to your wife/husband/family and leave me alone. I suspect they're secretly blaming each other for their current situation — being stuck in a campsite — so I play a mental game, looking at their body language to deduce which one of them had the idea of going camping this summer.

Then there's the sight of seeing men washing up plastic plates in communal sinks. I can't explain why, but there's something about it that just seems pitiful. How can this be better than relaxing at home? How bad must their homes be?

If you ever go on the run for a crime you did or didn't commit, don't try staying under the radar by going from campsite to campsite in France. You'll find yourself 'fessing up to the allegations whether you're guilty or not.

I finally climb all four terraces and reach the showers. There are only three cubicles to choose from. All of them are in use, two of them with parents washing their kids. I wait and wait. My arse is killing and I remove the cotton wool pad, which now smells like it's rotting. Finally, I'm able to have a wash.

After my shower I'm really at a low ebb. A nice lady in the pitch opposite gestures to say we can use her line as I hang up my washing, but I'm at the point of no return, slowly reaching the bottom of my pit of despair. I say no, we're OK thanks, before diving in the tent as 'welling up' becomes 'breaking through'.

I well up every now and then, probably a lot more since having children. It's rarely if ever because of self-pity, more often when I see or read about beautifully moving acts of kindness or selflessness.

The last time I felt actual tears roll down my cheeks, though, was when Manda miscarried, a couple of years after we married. She had only been pregnant for seven or eight weeks, so it was very early, but as a young couple we were excited and the baby was planned. In the end, we spent the night at A&E in East Surrey Hospital, among drunks and druggies — one idiot even took a whizz up against the back of our chairs while we were waiting — just to be told by a doctor whose English wasn't top notch that we'd "aborted the baby". Not the most tactful way to break the news.

We left the hospital, got back in the car and I rang mum and dad. That's when I broke down and cried. I suppose, like now I was tired. At that moment I also realised that I'd had a charmed life, but nobody is always lucky. Looking back on it now, and knowing the boys were to pop out a year later, it's easy to believe that things do all happen for a reason. But it was the kind of time where I wished mum and dad were on the same landmass.

In any case, what's happening to me right now really isn't quite so serious. I'm just stuck half-way down the middle of France, in a tent, with my bike, in excruciating pain, away from home, with at least four days to go.

Matt's quiet so I head off to the showers. On one of the trips to do my washing — a daily task to ensure that we not only smell relatively fresh, but also keep our cycling shorts in good fettle and free of dangerous diseases — I hear a young lad in one of the toilet cubicles swearing violently because he cannot find any toilet paper. It is actually in a gigantic drum attached to the cubicle wall. I think he finds it eventually, but I continue with my washing and leave soon afterwards.

Dad comes back from the shower and it's time to eat. I open up my pannier and, sweet Lord, my undercarriage must be worse than I thought. Even though I'm cleaning my kit every day there's an awful whiff coming from my clothes bag. I hunt through, trying to find the offending pair of shorts or pants only to realise the old chap has very generously decided to stow away last night's half-eaten saucisson in my bag and the aroma it produces is exactly the same as the juices secreted by my fetid nethers. Nice one.

It's only a brief moment of hilarity.

I hold it together while we eat, but by the time we phone home I really can't speak to mum or Manda. I text Manda instead and try to sleep.

Lying in the dark, I hear somebody nearby take out a guitar.

FFS, as they say.

Thought for the day: The most useless thing I've learnt on this trip is that the word 'immobilière' is French for estate agent. Trust me, I won't ever need to know that.

RIDES OF PASSAGE

DAY 7
Family Cycling

Saturday August 20, 1994 — Lubersac to Saint Céré (65 miles)
Saturday August 8, 2015 — Saint Yrieix to Vayrac (66.8 miles)

Matt aged 15

I woke at 6am but Dad said it was really misty so I stayed in bed until 7am. All our stuff hanging out to dry was soaked so we stuck it to the back of the bike.

We left the campsite at 8.15am and rode up a long hill to Arnac. Dad cut his leg on his pedal so he plastered that up.

We had breakfast at Objat - pains aux raisins. Here they were setting up a fair like that at Lubersac. After Objat we had a long run in a valley floor to Brive, where the road resembled a race track. Dad got something stuck in his eye here and after a short while I managed to break another spoke.

We spent half an hour fixing that and left Brive on the quickest road possible. This was steep and took us to Noailles. We took a small road to Nazareth where Dad knocked on a tabac door only to find a family eating their lunch inside.

We continued to Turenne, which is an ancient town up on a hill. Then we followed a huge descent down to the Dordogne. A passing Frenchman took a photo of both of us on a bridge over the river.

In Bretenoux we bought a sausage, water, pains au chocolat, white wine, red wine, tomatoes, peaches, tins of tuna salad, sardines and bread. Then we finished with a 9km ride to Saint Céré which is low in a valley. We arrived at the campsite by 5.30pm.

For tea we had the white wine, bread, some tuna salad, tomatoes, peaches, sardines, pains au chocolat and chocolate. We put the wine in the river to cool it.

We phoned Mum, had a drink, wrote our journals and went to sleep.

Today has been a really boiling day with some huge hills. Unfortunately, in the background I can see even bigger hills we need to climb tomorrow. I am feeling quite good and rode well but the sight of the hills is depressing. Dad bought an adjustable spanner today. He has been struggling all day due to not eating lunch.

Today we rode 104.6km. We went to sleep at 10.30pm.

Arthur aged 42

Made good speed into Juillac, despite big climbs out of Lubersac to Arnac-Pompadour. Levelled out and went well until we started to climb again after Brive le Gaillarde. Another blessed spoke broke there. Had a huge climb out of there to Noailles, walked all the way.

Another big climb to Turenne, which was very touristy. Interrupted a family having lunch in their dining room at Nazareth (Matt assured me it was a tabac!).

Long descent from Turenne to Turenne le Gare. Flat thereafter through Vayrac, Quatre Routes (fruit and more water) to Bretonneux (two soft drinks) and then to Saint Céré.

Bought food for two days in Saint Céré as everything is shut on Sunday. Also bought an adjustable spanner in case of freewheel removal.

Highlights of the day:

— Scraped my leg when my pedal slipped.
— Huge hills / boiling hot.
— Massive load of wet washing again.
— Broke more spokes (five).
— Brive le Gaillarde is a grand prix.
— Hard work — bonked 30km from our destination.
— Saint Céré good campsite — hot showers.

Matt aged 36

After three or four days of waking at 6am, today we get up at 7.30am. There was a massive storm overnight and the rain was pelting down until about 7. I take the opportunity to really stretch my legs before getting up. I've been using hydration tabs with my water, which help replace salts and avoid cramp. I'm not a big fan of sports nutrition but I fully recommend hydration or electrolyte tabs. One thing I've noticed about getting older is that cramp can hit much more often, but these tabs really keep it at bay. However, they can't do anything about the lactic acid in your legs come morning. So part of my daily routine on this trip has been to repeatedly stretch and tense my quads as soon as I wake. It's a bizarre sensation — you can almost feel the lactic sloshing about in the muscles. At least my potential hip problem of a few days ago has passed with a little bit of tweaking to my saddle height.

We finally get up, dress and set off quickly. Dad seems to be under the impression that our clothes will dry on the back of the bike, despite the fact I keep telling him the weather is going to be like this for a couple of days. Ho hum.

We head out of Saint Yrieix, following the same road to the supermarket that we never reached last night. Blimey, if that's two minutes as the sign says, what were they travelling in? (Le) Concorde? We head on through a village called Glandon, then enjoy a fun little snaking descent through the trees. Obviously there's a heaving great climb the other side, but the drop at least puts a smile on my face. Our first big stop of the day will be at Ségur le Château: an olde worlde town and dad's clearest memory — it's looking increasingly like one of our few reliable memories — from 1994.

Sure enough we reach Ségur and it hasn't changed in 21 years. In fact, you can put a nought on the end of those 21 years and that sentence would still be right. I pop into the general store and buy us some breakfast food: pains au chocolate, etc, as per usual. We sit on a wall in a restaurant car park, just over a bridge, trying to find some shelter under a huge tree while we eat. Some bloke appears at an upstairs window at the restaurant and makes a big show of playing with a cat. They probably don't see many people round here, he might as well make the most of it, and he duly does. Odd sod.

Arthur aged 63

Ségur le Château sits on a narrow river called L'Auvézère. It is feted as one of 'France's Pretty Villages', and deservedly so. Most of the houses look like they went up in the 14th Century and it has a particular untouched charm about it. I reprise some photos that we had taken during our last visit in 1994.

Despite the rain getting worse, we have to press on. The one upside is that the rain is not very cold. I put a Buff on my head so that the water doesn't run into my eyes, but for most of the time there's not much to see around us except for nondescript greyness. That said, one of the benefits of the rain appears to be that the sunflowers now have their heads up and are looking at us. Over the past few days, the heat has made them hang their heads downwards, like statues at a war memorial.

We've got some big carriageways coming up ahead, so we should also make the most of these relatively quiet roads. But the rain is falling hard again and my backside is hurting more than at any point since Argenton. I start thinking about home.

I've never particularly liked leaving home at the best of times, and I know everybody loves their kids — yada yada yada — but I have a particular attachment to my boys because, since they were nine months old, I've been the person who has stayed at home to look after them.

It's a deal whereby I'm absolutely the winner. I hated the compulsion of having to go into an office every Monday to Friday. At the same time, Manda is an incredible woman, and despite being the headteacher of a large and busy junior school, as soon as she comes home she is very definitely mummy. I've never heard her say anything about being the main breadwinner or having to go out to work, or needing any 'me' time. In fact, the idea of 'me' time is something of an anathema to both of us.

But I've been the one who has always taken the boys to school, picked them up, and amused them until teatime. Any book or magazine writing or editing has had to be done during naps when they were babies, at night, or when they're at school. Even when I've done jobs away from home, I've always taken Manda and the boys with me.

So now I'm going to talk about having children. It's a hugely controversial subject. But I don't care, this is my book, I'm going to do it anyway.

The first time I can remember the issue of us having children being raised publicly, we were at a meal out with friends. Some people we all knew had just had a baby, and before this child was born it had already been booked into a nursery. I understand that's the way things have to be sometimes. What Manda and I found less palatable, though, was that this particular couple's older child was also in childcare each day. Yet it was July and the people we were talking about were teachers on their summer holidays.

What were they doing that meant they couldn't see their children, we wondered?

They were spending each day at the beach, surfing.

We couldn't understand why anyone would have children if they didn't want to see them, especially during the summer holidays? (At this point I have to blame my current companion on this trip for many of my views. Mum stopped work to look after me when I was born, and neither she or dad would go to so much as a wedding unless we were all invited as a family.)

So, at this meal, I can remember there were tears and tantrums — not from us, I hasten to add — as others round the table, who had done very similar things with their children, told us we didn't know what we were talking about; we'd never had children; we should shut up; it's different when you have kids, etc. Somebody else piped up and said — without any knowledge of our personal finances — he couldn't see how we could afford for one of us to stop working to look after any children we were planning to have.

But we'd done our maths — family planning doesn't have to just be about condoms and contraception — and I was certain that with a tightening of belts it could be done. Simply put, we were prepared. We weren't necessarily prepared for twins, of course. But, in any case, you get roughly nine month's warning before a baby — or babies — pop out.

After the miscarriage we waited a year to try again. Manda thoroughly loved being pregnant, she was still playing hockey until about six months gone, and she ended up being about as wide as she was tall. The birth itself was relatively traumatic; the all-round hospital experience is something I never want to repeat. And the memory of driving home with the boys in the car for the first time is one that will never leave me. I might as well have had a Ming vase balanced precariously on the roof. I don't think we went above 20mph the whole way.

It was almost as delicate a journey as I'm trying to survive now.

Dad and I reach the top of the hill out of Ségur. The main town on our route today is Brive la Gaillarde, a place we remember well from 1994 because we ended up going freestyle with the route on that occasion, too. The roads into Brive were little more than a racetrack, so I've had to plan around not getting too close today. Even so, we can't afford to avoid some big 'D' roads entirely.

The rain is really pelting down and I take a picture of dad in his waterproof jacket. We have stopped among fields of cider apples but that brings back a bitter taste after yesterday's exploding bottle. We desperately try to wipe the water off our glasses but it's next to no use. Almost everything we have to wipe them is equally sodden. I also realise that with current power levels I can no longer have both my phone's Strava app and my GPS recording our route, so I turn off the GPS.

Despite the rain today, we're probably doing our fastest speeds all trip. At times it is like a two-up time trial as we battle against the elements. It feels like we are a team riding together. Matt and I have ridden alongside each other quite a lot over the years. As well as our first French trip we raced mountain bikes together, we even took part in a pedallo challenge at Centre Parcs once, although that ended up with us getting beached on an island in the middle of the boating lake.

I tried to be involved as much as I could when Matt and his brother Richard were young. I went to all the 'meet the teacher' events, but as I worked on Saturdays I did not attend what could often be the agony of school football matches. I was usually there for the Cub Scout football on a Sunday afternoon, though. This was very character-building for everyone involved, as they only ever won one match.

The journey from childhood to manhood has various points that are common to many boys, one of which is time spent as a Cub or a Scout. Both Matthew and Richard did Cubs and my role, right from the start, was to go along to make sure nothing happened to them.

Naturally, being something of an outdoorsy type, I was happy to do this. It certainly was an experience on several fronts, but the most surprising thing was undoubtedly the amount of wine that was drunk by the leaders. I can only imagine that it was consumed as an antidote to the out-of-control bunch of brats that these saints had volunteered to look after for the weekend.

When Richard became a Cub, Susan very gamely joined the ranks of the leaders as there was a dire shortage at the time (in truth, the parents were all but blackmailed to sign up). In so doing, she let me off the hook for the odd weekend, although it must be said that I still went along to most camps. Susan was given a uniform which, even with her inside, did little to flatter. It was worse for the other leaders, who in the main resembled sumo wrestlers and who must have tested the seams to breaking point.

One of the more memorable trips was a weekend in Alderney, the most northerly of the Channel Islands. The majority of the kids were issued with BMX bikes to ride around on. The bloke in the local hire shop must have thought it was his birthday because he was actually building more bikes for us as we waited.

He did not always have enough bolts to do the job, sadly, which is something that came home to me when I tried to do what is called a 'kerb endo'. This is an easy stunt, it simply requires you to pull on the front brake and move your body forward so that the back wheel rises a foot or so into the air. It might be impressive to the layman but it doesn't need a vast amount of skill on the rider's part.

Sadly, I had chosen one of the bikes that was short on bolts. In fact it had only three bolts securing the handlebars and not four, and these were not too tight either. So when I cycled up to do my party piece and I applied the front brake, the handlebars shot forward and I was forced to leap over the front of the bike in as casual fashion as I could muster. Whether or not the audience believed that it was the default option of a kerb endo, I shall never know, but I did no further cycling that weekend.

It's no excuse, of course, but I felt I could take something of a backseat when it came to child rearing because Matt and Richard had their mother at home all of the time. This is something that Susan and I believed was quite important. More important, in fact, than having 20 television sets around the house or five holidays a year. Of course, I accept that we may be wrong, but so far it seems like our two sons have become happy, balanced individuals, which to us is the ultimate purpose of parenthood.

This sounds all very serious and parenthood should not be serious at all. There is plenty of other serious stuff going on in the world without adding more into your life. But I have to admit that I spent a great deal of my time at work, and for years I was a serial hobbyist, so my appearance was usually at dinner times and my two days off each week. In truth, I don't know if anything can prepare you for parenthood. It is such a surprising, enchanting and occasionally frustrating voyage, that no one can foresee or indeed answer all the questions that pop up.

After that attack of profoundness, let's lighten the mood a bit. Every one knows that a small child's vocabulary is limited, and words that are foreign to most people actually mean something to the doting parents. Matthew used to visit my dad from time to time, and my dad was always delighted to offer him a glass of lemonade and a biscuit. This used to send a shudder up our spines as dad's was not the cleanest house around, so we dreaded Matt shouting out 'goom and gaga bibis' ('drink and chocolate digestive biscuit please') to my dad, who by then knew what he meant.

Parenthood doesn't even get easier as the years pass. By the time your prodigy have reached their teens, school gets serious and drink and girlfriends appear on the scene. Then they go to university, far, far away, where they have to stand on their own two feet and there's nothing that you can do even if you wanted to.

So get a dog. It's like an eternal small child and at least you know what it's up to at 4 o'clock on a Sunday morning.

In other circumstances this would be great cycling territory. The road is smooth and relatively flat — in fact, we're looking at pretty much a constant descent to Brive this morning — but in these conditions it's hard to enjoy it. Then we spot a sign that says 38km to Brive. Sweet lordy.

Day 7 — Family Cycling

Far closer, only 7km away is the town of Juillac. We aim for that.

This road is certainly quick and we're haring along at almost dangerous speeds. Between the sweat and rain water running into my eyes, and the droplets flicking onto my glasses, visibility is next to nothing. Juillac comes as a blessed relief. We drop down towards the town and find shelter under a bus stop.

Dad and I sit down and chat. One thing you have to say about the old chap is that he's never been big on preaching to us. The only mantras for life I can ever remember him coming out with are: "There's only one standard: A1," which I suppose he used to promote the idea of excellence (although it rather comes from the "There's no 'I' in 'team'" school of profundity); and "If it feels good, do it." That last offering is a pretty odd thing to tell children and must have come from the *Dr Way-Too-Jolly Book of Child Care* or *The Cheech and Chong Guide to Counter Intuitive/Double Bluff Parenting*. In any case, it seems to have worked. Neither me nor my brother Ritchie smoke, drink to excess (very often), or have a crack addiction.

But dad is quietly impressive in a number of ways. I'm conscious I haven't chatted much about dad so far on this journey. The truth is, we haven't really chatted much ourselves so far. It's been so hard, and we've been so tired that we've been more like company rather than ride companions. But he just keeps going and going, and that in itself is inspiration enough. If you get your ideas of how people should behave from your parents, one important life skill in my eyes is the notion of simply getting on with things without complaint.

I certainly didn't complain when Manda went back to work after nine months of looking after the boys and I took over full-time daycare duties. Although, I can remember somebody once saying to me: "But won't stopping work affect your idea of yourself as a man?"

I found that a pretty odd statement.

First of all, I'm a writer, so I'm sort of working all the time — I don't need to go into an office to prove it. Secondly, that question has strangely caveman-ish overtones to it. I'm over six foot tall, I weigh 16 stone, I've trained with the army, I've been an international rifle shooter, captain of the school rugby team and I've played in a rock and roll band. Whatever stereotypes of manliness you subscribe to, I reckon I would fulfill a fair few of them. In any case, at the time I was more concerned with proving my ability as a dad.

So the plan was to survive on Manda's wage and I'd just concentrate on the boys. But within a month or two I had an email from a Japanese gentleman who owned a book company. He had read something I'd written in *Cycle Sport* magazine about Lance Armstrong and wanted to know if I'd author a book about Lance to tie in with the American's 2008 comeback. A few weeks later I met this Japanese chap at Costa Coffee in Piccadilly, and the book *Lance and Le Tour* was born.

Over the next four months I looked after the boys when they were awake, and scheduled interviews with Armstrong's former team-mates for when they were asleep. I'd spend mornings at library rhyme time, or a play group, or even 'Legs, Bums and Mums'. (Yes, I went once and they almost killed me — sexism is alive and well among women, too. I was made to do full press-ups while everybody else did half-arsed efforts on their knees. I know they'd all just had babies, but blokes tend to put on a bit of timber once they're married with kids, too.) Then in the afternoon I'd be chatting to George Hincapie or Viatcheslav Ekimov. I remember one particular occasion where I had a boy on each knee and I was trying to get through to interview Union Cycliste Internationale president Pat McQuaid. That interview never happened, although it wasn't because of the boys.

Lance and Le Tour is not the most fantastic piece of cycling journalism ever. I certainly tried my best to look at Armstrong's seven Tour de France victories afresh and I interviewed a host of people close to him to get their personal memories from each edition of the race. The general atmosphere among British cycling journalists at the time was very hostile towards Armstrong. However, as a one-man band with no legal protection of a major media company behind me, I couldn't afford to take any risks: Lance wasn't shy to sue.

Of course, the sad thing we know now is that the whole concept was built around a grand lie and *Lance and Le Tour* could be called my first — unwitting — work of fiction. I keep hoping I can go to watch the pulping of the remaining unsold copies.

Funnily enough, during the course of writing *Lance and Le Tour* I got to within a whisker of interviewing both Floyd Landis and Tyler Hamilton only a short time before they revealed their doping-with-Lance back-stories to the world, which eventually brought about his downfall. What would I have done with those kind of testimonies had they been revealed to me? I honestly don't know, but it would have been stressful.

Am I bitter that Lance cheated? No, we all expected it. If you're going to write about pro cycling you'd have to be a fool to believe everything you're writing will remain true for time immemorial. Pro cycling mags are less a case of tomorrow's chip paper and more tomorrow's legal document. A suspension of disbelief should be a requisite for any cycle racing fan.

What affected me more — although I never lost any sleep about it — was that I was personally lied to by a great many of the charming people who I interviewed while putting the book together. It's one thing to be duped along with the masses, it's quite another to have people lie to you in a one-on-one conversation. But I suspect for the people concerned, the fact they told me a few porkies is the least of the things they need to feel ashamed about.

Nowadays I don't write anything about pro cycle racing and I read very little about it. When I do see something, I'm invariably left worrying at the innocence with which many people in Britain view bike racing again. I don't have such faith, mainly because there's hardly ever been a time when cycle racing was clean. From brandy-and-arsenic concoctions, laying tacks on the road and catching trains in the early days; to micro-dosing, very possibly genetic doping and hidden electric motors right now, it's a sport with a long and infamous history of cheating. The continual doping cases that still rear their heads tend to support that view.

From a personal point of view, though, I am proud of *Lance and Le Tour*. Being able to write a book while also being a full-time dad to one-year-old twin boys is quite an achievement, even if the book itself has become redundant. These days, when people tell me how hard others work, I take it with a pinch of salt.

Having a back catalogue of experiences like that, along with dad's resolution to keep going at least quietens the voice inside my head which keeps saying I can't cycle much further. I'm not sure I can see the end of this journey anywhere within reach, but I know each little step, each town passed through, is a little bit closer towards success. That means we have to leave Juillac.

We've been keeping an eye on the visibility of a church steeple over the roofs to see if conditions are getting any better, but they're not. We've also been talking about possible bail-out options for later today, considering where nearer campsites might be. I suspect, though, we'll just keep going and going until we can't go any more.

Back on the road, the weather does seem to ease and at least rain isn't falling quite so hard any more. We're also making incredibly good time. The old chap has taken to the front like a steam train, powering along these flat roads with me in tow. Although our physiologies are fairly different, relatively speaking — he's a rake, I'm, er, not — we're actually well matched and miles fly by in a sodden blur. We chuff through the town of Objat and have to follow diversion signs but there's no stopping the Lamy Express.

As the road nears Brive the amount of heavy vehicles passing us markedly increases. It's not a massive problem because I have a plan to take us away from the hubbub and circumvent Brive around its south-western edge. All these route changes are a gamble and we'll never really know if they pay off. Often, it's a case of going for perceived safety over easier or shorter routes.

How much energy would we save just going in a direct line? We'll never find out. But if we can at least get to Sète in one piece, I suppose we shouldn't feel too hard done-by.

We branch off to the right, heading for Saint Pantaleon de Larche — the patron saint of baggy trousers and conifers — and then on to Larche itself. Certainly this seems like a good route. It's flat, moderately quiet and gently curves alongside the easy waters of La Vazère river. With hills visible either side, it's a pleasant option. For all the dull-grey greenery around us, I'm aware we're in a more urban area than we have been in so far today. There are bigger roads within sight, and each town has the strange feeling of being a satellite to Brive. Meanwhile, dad's efforts this morning have started to catch up with him and he's dropping back a little. He doesn't have to go much further. Eventually our route takes us over a bridge and we enter Larche, our planned lunch stop.

It's been a pretty boring session so far today and, with our minds able to wander, we've actually made fairly decent progress by the time we stop for lunch at a nondescript town called Larche. Before we eat, I station myself at the side of the road while Matt goes to the chemist to search for something to repair his bum. I must look like a local because one motorist stops to ask me the way to wherever. Naturally, I cannot help him. Hopefully, the four panniers hanging on my bike and the sleeping mat on my rear carrier will give him a clue that I am not from 'round these parts'.

It is a good place to stop. I am on a crossroads and the amount of cars that go one way, come back again, and go off another way is impressive. As I wait, I count five mosquito bites about my person, and make a mental note to camp away from water in future.

I take a very brief look around Larche. There's a small general store but around the corner I see a sign for a boulangerie, so I decide to walk as far. Even by French standards it's an odd set-up. Having passed so many closed shops, I know they're not particularly keen on serving people, but this baker's has vertically-slatted blinds preventing anyone from even seeing the goods on display. The last time I saw anything similar, the establishment in question was a sex shop. ("Is this a sex shop? I'll have a fiver's worth please.")

I have other pressing matters, too. We're almost out of Healing Gel and things aren't getting any better where the sun doesn't shine — which is pretty much everywhere at the moment. Luckily, there's a pharmacy. Although, I suspected there would be. C'est la France.

Food can wait, the underworld is calling so the chemist comes first. Inside I explain my predicament in halting French to a very charming and very pretty young lady. If I was to adhere to the old joke, I would end up leaving only with a tube of toothpaste. But this is no laughing matter. She speaks to me in quick French and recommends an antiseptic cream for the evening, and a skin soothing cream for the morning. I apologise for my poor language skills but she smiles and says it's fine, she can speak English but she didn't feel there was any need. I'm touched (not literally, mind) by the whole experience.

Rather less moving is a visit to the mini-mart over the road. I try to get plenty of food and water but it's not France's finest deli we're dealing with here. Still, there's just about enough to keep us going.

Our next point of interest is a town called Turenne. It's built on the side of a hill and we have a picture of it from last time. It's a fair way away and we've got some climbing to do. Quite how much climbing, I never realised from our map, but it's essentially 10 miles of constant uphill. It does have a few things going for it, though. First of all, the way is very scenic and for the first portion we have a beautiful view of a lake down to our left, with small hills beyond. The second thing is that the slope is constant and at a gradient that I quite enjoy. It reminds me of cycling up the easier side of the Bwlch-y-Groes, the highest road in Wales, which I did as 'hill-climbing for fatties' feature in *Cycling Active* magazine. Physically, I was the obvious candidate, and luckily I was also *CA's* chief writer.

Helping to launch *Cycling Active* was great fun. For me, it started in a soft play centre with the boys. They must have been about 18 months old at the time and I remember getting a call on my mobile from Robert Garbutt, then editor of *Cycling Weekly*. He said they were thinking about starting a monthly magazine and would I write for it. Working with Garbutt is like being in the army, you try to never volunteer for anything but eventually he always gets you to say yes. It proved to be a good move. Within a few years, with very little promotion, we were IPC Media's biggest selling monthly cycling mag. More to the point, I could write the cycling stories I had always wanted to write without compromise.

My goal with the original version of *Cycling Active* (the magazine has since had a rebranding) was to bridge the gap between cycling and normal, daily life. I went out riding with famous faces to find out the simple benefits that cycling brought them; I dressed up in silly costumes and spoofed TV shows and books to show the kind of cycling-inspired fun it's possible to have without shying away from popular culture; I met with real people whose lives had been transformed, for the better, by hopping on their bikes.

The rise of the MAMIL created an interested new audience that soaked up these messages, at least initially. Sadly, I know a lot of MAMILs have forgotten that originally for them cycling was a passport to new experiences, and have become as trenchant about certain things as old-school roadies. Some have restructured their lives around their bikes and become as obsessive about pedalling as they had previously been about their careers, or golf, or DIY.

I've also heard plenty of MAMILs trot out that old line about how a three-hour morning ride gives them so much energy to play with their kids for the rest of a Sunday. I think that's nonsense. They're just addicted to pushing their legs round. That's fine, and I understand that everybody needs a break from life at times. But don't be a hypocrite. By the time you've got your bike ready, left home, done three hours cycling possibly with an hour-long coffee stop en route, then got back, put the bike away and had a shower, there's sweet Fanny Adams left of Sunday to do much. And you're probably in no fit state to do it anyway.

Just say you like riding your bike and leave it at that — nobody will hold it against you. As I've said, I'm not like a normal cyclist. On Sunday I'd rather have a lie-in and then play with my kids.

In fact, the lengths these people go to to tell you how much cycling improves their family life should light up a beacon. One thing I've learnt since having children is that most parents instinctively know what's wrong or right for their families. I know this because of the pains they take to explain themselves when secretly they suspect they've made a bad choice. (As an aside, while I absolutely do believe any parent who says they would be prepared to sacrifice their life for their child, I think being prepared to sacrifice your lifestyle makes far more of a statement.) Having children is a guilt trip from beginning to end, and those feeling the most guilt often also feel the need to confess. There's no way you can make the right decision every single time. But if you find yourself having to publicly over-explain one of your actions, that's the red flag that it might be wrong.

In my case, if I find myself making some prolonged justification about some choice I've made, the easiest thing is to instantly rethink my decision. That means I've turned down some incredible jobs in recent years — things most cyclists would give their eye-teeth for. But equally, if the boys become mass murderers in 20 years' time, I at least want to say, hand on heart, I really did try my best.

With all this in mind, I can't help feeling that my tears last night were actually the realisation that I might have made the wrong choice about doing this trip. Perhaps I should have spent two weeks enjoying the summer holidays with Manda and the boys instead. But again, this trip is a bit like raising a family: it's a series of small steps and achievements. The difference is, I'm far keener to get to the end of this specific, literal journey than the longer, metaphorical one.

After lunch and Larche we face a couple of hours of climbing. The views are good, which is some consolation. We do a reprise photo as we near Turenne, an old hill top town. While we are stopped a Citroen Light 15 passes us, decorated with white ribbons and which clearly has a bride and groom inside. Following it is a wedding cavalcade of countless cars. Seemingly the whole of France has been invited and they're tooting their car horns avec gusto.

After all the climbing we've done since lunch it means we can enjoy some descent and there's a really nice drop to the floor of the Dordogne Valley. I'm finding it hard to get a sense of perspective about these geographical features. I mean, I think of valleys back in Jersey and England, which can only be a fraction of the size of this, but in my mind they seem so similar.

We're on flat, straight roads now and we're making good time. However, the old chap is wilting a little and our electronic power supplies are low, too. For all the clackety-clack cacophony coming from my dynamo, the rain seems to have got into the system and it's been unable to recharge my phone. Dad suggests we aim for Vayrac — about 15 miles short of our ideal goal Saint Céré — and look for a hotel today if we can. Mais, c'est la France.

It is a shame we can't quite reach Saint Céré, as this is the campsite dad has fondest memories of from back in '94. But we're simply not able to get there today and, for the first time on this trip, it almost feels like it's getting too dark to ride. That's due more to the blanket of thick cloud cover than a setting sun, though.

There's no sign of any hotels when we reach Vayrac, however, I do spot directions for the campsite. We decide to give these a whirl but reach a point with signs for camping on both sides of the road, and a distance of two kilometres given. I'm buggered if I'm going to ride a further two kilometres out of our way for a campsite, so we head back to centre ville and — as always in these circumstances — use precious power resources to phone home for assistance. A car filled with a half-witted family pulls up while I chat to Manda and the teenage muppets in the back take the micky out of us in English from their open window. Maman et papa chuckle along as well. That's nice.

Manda looks up hotels in the area but there's precious little. However, she says the municipal campsite is very close. We head back towards the confusing signs, stopping in a boulangerie to stock up on drinks. The nice lady there says the campsite is only a hundred metres down the road — the 2km sign is for a private campsite further on.

We've wasted more time again, just like yesterday, and find the municipal site not far from where we turned back an hour ago. Again, it's depressing and not really our fault, just another situation caused by poor signage.

We pay at the campsite Portacabin and pick a pitch. It's not raining any more but everything is soaked. Compared to yesterday, though, I'm in heaven. It's a wide open site with no terraces; there's nobody in your face 'bonjouring'; there are kids kicking a football; music is playing quietly out of a radio; and everything feels very relaxed and normal. We are given a key for the toilets and showers, and the lady who signs us in says we can use the power supplies inside the wash block to recharge our equipment.

After putting up the tent, I go for a wash and enjoy a far longer shower than yesterday. There's no queue, in fact there's nobody else in the block at all. I treat the areas that need to be treated and start the new regime of antiseptic cream. I've also plugged my iPhone into a power socket high up on the wall by the sinks. I know dad won't use it — not unless he can sit there looking at it to make sure nobody half inches it — but I'm quite content to leave the phone charging while I have a wash. In the end, it is for nought — for some reason it won't charge. I suspect my power lead has been somehow compromised by the rain, especially as it doesn't seem to work with the power bank I have back in the tent either. Pooh, I'll need to find somewhere that sells iPhone leads now.

As I walk back to the tent I'm stopped by a charming French man — an obvious cyclist judging by his physique — who is intrigued by our bikes and general get-up. I explain what we're doing and he is even more impressed. We chat for a little while about bikes, bike racing, Bernard Hinault and Lance Armstrong. I have to say we've yet again met the full extremes of French folk today, from the wonderful to the obnoxious.

We are getting desperate for some electricity to charge our various pieces of tech. The woman at reception suggests that we plug them in at the shower block. However, because it means leaving your stuff charging unattended or standing guard over it, I abandon the idea.

It is another rather damp evening, but we do our usual chores and retire early. In my efforts to swallow my gigantic anti-inflammatory tablets, I inadvertently tip a litre bottle of water in the tent. Luckily Matt is away having a shower and I quickly mop it up as best I can.

The tent is designed to be waterproof, especially from the ground beneath it, so there was no chance that it would drain out anywhere. In fact, so effective is it that you could probably make a very good covered duck pond if you filled it up with water.

As I suspect, I'm right about dad and the plug socket. He can't bring himself to leave his £80 Samsung phone charging while he has a shower a full three feet away, so there's an opportunity to restock on power missed. He also has another attack of weirdness at tea, hacking a full inch off the end of the saucisson — yes, that dreaded puss-smelling saucisson strikes again — because it might have "gone bad" since yesterday.

I get stroppy and tell him we need to eat, and I hardly think a saucisson — which after all is just squashed together random bits of God-knows-what — is likely to do him a mischief. He doesn't relent, so I grab the piece he's about to throw away and eat it. It's one thing him not being particularly interested in food, quite another watching him willfully chucking it away. We have a far less controversial raspberry tart for pudding.

I'm nowhere near as fed-up as yesterday and this evening I can bring myself to chat to everybody at home. With limited power I can't do much about surfing the web to plan tomorrow's route, so I study our paper maps for a long time instead. There is some serious climbing coming up. We hang washing out to dry but I'm pretty sure it'll be wetter in the morning than it is now. Everything is soaking.

All across France in years to come, will there be bibshorts hanging on trees as tributes to the unknown cycle tourists?

Thought for the day: If France had as many (open) grocers as they have pharmacies, they might not need so many multi-vitamins.

DAY 8
More Cowbell

**Sunday August 21, 1994 — Saint Céré to Marcillac
(58.7 miles)
Sunday August 9, 2015 — Vayrac to Decazeville
(51.4 miles)**

Matt aged 15

I woke up at 7am and we managed to leave Saint Céré before 8.30am.

After only a short while we arrived at a huge climb. We got to the top surprisingly quickly by walking and cycling, taking loads of pictures on the way.

We got to Ayrac where we had breakfast, then we went on to Figeac where Dad bought me a soft drink and some water. To get to our next goal, Decazeville, we had to climb a huge hill and then rode down a descent that took us through a tunnel built out of stone.

Dad was struggling a bit now and the sun was hotter than ever so we stopped every 10km. Eventually we got to Decazeville but everything was shut so we had nothing to eat. After a little break we went on to Firmi, which was like a new town although everything was shut again. However, we managed to fill our bottles with drinking water. After going on for a little longer we reached a bar. Here we had two Kronenbourgs.

We went quickly after that for some way but Dad was dying. We had two small pains au chocolat and decided not to go to Rodez and found a campsite in Marcillac instead.

I set the tent up quickly while Dad went to get some food. He got us four cold cans, two bottles of water, two jesuits (pastry things) and two baguettes.

Soon afterwards a storm appeared which absolutely chucked it down. We then had a shower and tea which was the baguettes, two salad tuna things, duck pâté, the jesuits, tomatoes, rosé wine (which was horrible), and a bit of choccy. We then went to phone Mum. After that we wrote our journals, etc. We went to sleep at 9.30pm. Our campsite is quite nice, we have our own little area surrounded by bushes, although there is a rat right near our tent.

Tomorrow we have to go up some huge mountains, I am not looking forward to it, neither is Dad I think. We hope to wake at 6am so as to get a good start.

We travelled 94.5km in total today.

Arthur aged 42

Big climb out of Saint Céré — we walked. Fairly hard day, certainly for me, grovelling the last few kilometres. Very, very hot. Actually sweat dripping off us at 08.30hrs. Heat knackered me and I struggled most of the day. Finally gave in around 15.00hrs and went into a bar for two Kronenbourg each.

This killed the pain for half a mile or so, and then it was shafted time. Went through Saint Christophe, no campsite, so took left hand turning to Marcillac.

Reasonably good campsite. Just as well we stopped as a thunderstorm set in. Quickly put up tent in time. Fiery rosé wine for tea, did not drink it all. Very knackered today.

Highlights of the day:
— Sweating profusely at 08.30hrs.
— Nice tarte au pruneaux at Ayrac.
— Some huge descents and accompanying climbs.
— Good bike shop in Decazeville.
— No injuries or spoke breakages.
— Two Kronenbourgs = disaster.
— Had a rat next to us at the campsite.

Matt aged 36

For the second day running we awake to the sound of rain pelting the outside of our tent. And, just as I've recently learnt to be thankful for clouds and trees — those parts of nature that we don't often stop to appreciate — there is a comforting thrill about being under a thin layer of material, totally dry, while the heavens have opened above you.

So we don't bother to get moving too quickly. With nothing much to do, I try putting a bit more power back into my phone from my power pack. Would you believe it? It must have just been the damp getting into everything yesterday because my phone lead seems to be working again this morning. I top it up as best I can in the time we have before setting off.

Even after this small success we're still aiming for a hotel tonight. The reason why is all the more obvious after we poke our heads outside — all the clothing we dutifully washed last night is wetter than when we hung it up.

When the rain eases we finally get into routine. I follow my new treatment routine and apply skin-softening cream to the underworld. Then it's a case of packing bags and putting down the tent. The nice man I spoke to last night comes over and has a chat. We share email addresses. He wishes us good luck while we finish loading up the bikes.

Arthur aged 63

So far we have had no mechanical problems, no spoke breakages, no punctures, no road accidents and we have not been chased by any dogs either. In that regard, it's going a lot better than the last trip. I do, however, spend some time this morning checking our bikes. Matt's wheels are, like his saddle, completely new and untried, so it's no surprise then that one of his rear spokes is only finger tight. I tighten it and true the others, and take up the slack on his brakes. I do the same on my bike. We have cycled over 400 miles so some attention is needed.

While understandably the rigours of the road have made a little bike maintenance necessary, our hearts, lungs and legs are getting stronger with every pedal stroke. It might not feel that this is actually happening at all, but it's as true as the fact we are both developing the tan of the pro cyclist: brown arms up to the mid-bicep and brown legs from the mid-thigh down, but pasty white everywhere else.

Just before we depart we are buttonholed by a Frenchman who spoke to Matt last night and who is very impressed by our journey. He very nervously approaches us and asks for our autographs and email addresses. He seems a very nice chap, so we are happy to oblige, although I doubt if either of us really think that we rank anywhere near his other cycling idols.

We break camp and set off. After a short distance — by our current standards — we cross the Dordogne. Last time a friendly passerby took our photograph but on this occasion there is no one about, and actually this bridge is so tiny that it is rather a non-event. The scenery is interesting, though, because it appears that there is a mountain range on our left, and the tops of the mountains are covered in snow. I share this with Matt, but he thinks I am mistaking clouds for snow. He is right.

We're back on a pretty substantial 'D' road towards Saint Céré. But while planning our route last night I think I spotted what should be a more pleasant, quieter way and we branch off to the right. I'm going pretty well this morning, and the flat road suits my weight-handicapped abilities. The weather's still changeable, though, and we have to wear waterproofs while taking pictures of ourselves crossing the Dordogne.

There are plenty of campsites round here. It almost feels a shame we didn't go a bit further last night. That's the funny thing about this ride: at times I almost feel bitter towards yesterday's 'me' — why didn't I try a bit harder? Still, we're making good time and we soon approach the outskirts of Saint Céré. There's a serious amount of traffic out today — remember, this is a Sunday, holy folk — but it doesn't seem to be heading towards places of worship, preferring instead the bustling market in Saint Céré's centre ville.

We park the bikes up and I nip into a boulangerie for the usual selection of breakfast cakes, drinks and water. We don't hang about too long, we know there are some hills to come and we're not taking the cool conditions for granted.

I remember Saint Céré was the best campsite from our 1994 trip. Back then, I submerged our wine on the end of the washing line in the river and the shower block was exceptional. Today we never go near the campsite but cycle through the town only stopping to buy food.

Despite a relatively gentle start, the route out of Saint Céré goes continuously upwards. These small roads are delightful and the views are charming, but it becomes more and more unmistakably uphill. Matt seems to be suffering.

On our ride in 1994 we followed a big 'D' road south from Saint Céré but I'm keen to avoid it now. Instead, we'll try to follow as direct a route as possible, up to Latronquière and then down to Bagnac sur Célé. It's the same old compromise between safety and comfort, though. Our intended route seems to have a fair few up arrows on it, and if the spot heights nearby are to be believed, we'll be climbing from 250 feet to almost 2,000 feet in about 10 miles.

To say we're lulled into a false sense of security is an understatement. The route away from Saint Céré climbs only very gradually to start with. We stop by a pretty bridge and take some scenic portraits. Dad whips out his DSLR camera and starts moaning about his batteries being low. This must be the eighth time I've heard that a battery has run out on him, yet he's only brought four batteries. I ask him how this can be (partly because I'm fed up hearing it) and he explains he keeps putting old ones back in to eek out a bit of extra charge. I can understand the reasoning behind this process, what's harder to justify is his apparent surprise that a battery he knows has no charge indeed proves it has no charge left.

As I've said, dad's relationship with technology is a very odd one. He wanted to do a blog while we were away, posting online daily updates about how we were faring. Between a lack of Wifi at campsites and our own power issues, it hasn't come to pass. I'm not very keen on that idea anyway. I rather shrink away from social media — I only post anything on Facebook or Twitter if it means I can show off about interviewing somebody famous. Out of principle I take issue with giving words away for free.

That said, for my generation and every generation subsequently, computers are a natural part of life. I had the boys playing on the Nintendo Wii since they were about three. Is that good parenting? I reckon as long as you're with them, nothing done in moderation will do kids much harm.

For all that idealistic stuff I was spouting yesterday, don't think my life with my boys is an unbridled joyfest. They are two very competitive little chaps with uniquely well-matched abilities. In fact, you literally couldn't find two people who are any more similar as they share exactly the same DNA. That means when things get heated in competition — such as, say, a computer game — they get very heated. Add to that a general mischievousness and being a stay-at-home dad is hard work. I'd love to have worn a blood pressure monitor over the last eight years to see the highs it's hit and how long it stayed that way.

I always think it's funny when you read celebrities of a certain vintage who have had second families relatively late in life — for some reason, I'm thinking Des O'Connor here — and who say things like, "Oh yes, but having children keeps you young." I'm sure my two children have taken years off my life. Before they came along I was still in my twenties and almost had a full head of hair. Now I'm knocking on the door of middle-age and any hair that's left is slipping off the back of my bonce.

Possibly worse is that you see yourself grow into a dad — most often your own dad. I found myself using the old man's jokes the other day. We're selling our house, and I was showing a lady round who took a double look at one of our wedding photos. Seeing the handsome chap with long flowing locks, this potential buyer said incredulously: "My goodness is that you?"

I had to say: "Yes, but that was before I lost my hair from having the wife's thumb pushing down on the top my head." That's a pure Arf-ism. Meanwhile, the picture itself was very much a Dorian Gray moment. "How sad it is! I shall grow old, and horrible, and dreadful. But this picture will remain always young." The photo mocked me that day.

But nil desperandum. Dad and I are both still young enough to be taking on and just about beating this route across France. Right now the terrain is putting up its toughest fight yet, though. The climb up to Latronquière is baring its teeth and we're weaving up around the landscape. So far, so good, we've been able to put the bikes in a low gear and pedal — the old fella is climbing particularly well — but soon the slope hits sections of 12 per cent and we take to pushing, if only to give our legs a chance to shake out a bit of the lactic acid.

On sections like this the pain emanating from my saddle area seems to intensify. I just can't get back in a groove because I'm not able to pedal long enough to overcome the initial settling in phase. That we're travelling at a snail's pace does nothing to improve morale. The views are certainly impressive, though, with a rich tree-filled valley to our right. It all comes a bit too close for comfort on some sections, with the road edge becoming almost a sheer drop.

Our progress is slow. Very slow. It's the sort of climb you could probably have a good crack at on an unloaded carbon racing bike, but on heavy touring machines it's woeful. At least the weather has been cool and dry.

However, as we emerge from out of the tree line into more open, rolling, grass-covered hills the rain starts again. We're cold — that's a rarity on this trip — so it's on with the layers. The slope is still significant but it's definitely rideable, and we're keeping our legs ticking over. As we reach higher and higher up the hill we start to enjoy views on both sides. We must be getting nearer the top.

We turn left onto another big road, with Latronquière not much more than a mile away. I spot a 'Big Mat' building supplies merchant just outside the town and stop for a photo. Not only is it an obvious picture opportunity for me, but Big Mat have sponsored bike teams in the past and I have a matching Lycra cycling jersey at home.

We head towards the centre ville, although we can't discern if Latronquière really has one worth the name. In the end we park up outside some sort of municipal building opposite a tabac. We sit down on a wall at first, then retreat as far into the building's doorway as possible, attempting to get out of the drizzle while we eat lunch. Dad has to fix his bike because the brake blocks are rubbing on the wheel rim. I'm content — well, I don't know if content is the right word, but I've got to do something — to watch people going in and out of the tabac.

I think it's fair to say, without offending anybody any more than I already have, that there are some pretty odd characters in France. And the dodgiest of them seem to be going in and out of this bar. All trip I've been doppelganger spotting. I saw a Bradley Walsh-alike driving a van on the morning after Chasseneuil, and yesterday the Chuckle Brothers were in Larches. But this crew looks more like a cross between the cast of *The Last of the Summer Wine* and *The Walking Dead* (and I don't mean the living ones in that show). The thing is, they're looking at us as if we're weird.

We choose Latronquière as our lunch stop as it is literally the highest point of the day. The name sounds like this place should be some futuristic hub of technology but in fact it is just another washed-out village with boarded up shops and nobody around. I do a bit more maintenance on my bike, opening the rear brakes a touch and re-truing the back wheel. It was unlikely that there was anything wrong at all, but all that climbing begins to affect your mind, and any little rubbing noise takes on gargantuan proportions.

Once dad's happy with his bike, I'm keen to get going again. This has been our first proper mechanical delay — back in 1994 our memory seems to suggest they were happening all the time. I still wonder how we managed back then.

Lunch eaten and bike sorted we set off with the optimism of two blokes who think it is going to be all downhill from now on. It certainly seems that way initially, and after a short distance we stop because Matt has spotted an establishment called the Felix Club. It's severely tired out as a building, although it resonates with us because my other son, Richard, has a little boy called Felix.

My two sons are model fathers: they are at home a lot, they don't have all consuming pastimes that keep them away from the house, and they really cherish their offspring and their wives. I've always tried my best as a dad, although I would probably hold my hands up to the accusation of being a serial hobbyist.

Those hobbies, though, have never involved home improvements. But there is a reason for my DIY reticence (I have an excuse for everything so I'm told). Put simply, I like perfection or as close as I can get to it, but Susan just

144

wants the job done with the minimum of fuss. We reach common ground by staying with the status quo. It's cheap and there are no major upheavals.

I have been known to fit a tap washer, which I am reliably informed is not really house maintenance. And I can fit a plug, a light bulb and other easy stuff that does not take more than five minutes to carry out. Of course, there's also that old chestnut: 'How many cyclists does it take to change a light bulb?' The reply is: 'Three: One to fit it, and two to say how he could have done it better.' (Matt says the real answer is 'Six: One to fit it; two to say how he could have done it better; and three to stand around in WHSmith reading all about it in a cycling mag without actually buying a copy.')

Over a period of time, the amount of ridicule that has been projected in my direction by Mrs Lamy has certainly shown me to be as ordinary and fallible as anybody else, and in no way some superbeing whose word is law. We think that this is a healthy approach to family hierarchy, and it also puts me under no pressure, which is good, too. My dad was quite a distant figure and the absolute head of the house. From memory, he definitely was at home nearly all the time, but usually doing house painting or feverishly gardening. He had a green house and grew crops. He also kept chickens, which provided eggs and occasionally a chicken to eat.

As a young child, I remember seeing a headless chicken come running past me. There was no shock on my part. In fact, I was more amazed that the chicken knew where it was going without its head. After dispatching the poor bird, all that remained before cooking was to pluck it, which was surprisingly easy even for me. We would sit around a big barrel and pull out the feathers, letting them drop into the barrel. Today, all this sounds quite barbaric, but don't forget that my mum and dad had weathered the German Occupation of Jersey, when food was exceedingly scarce and if you did not grow it or raise it yourself, you went hungry.

As a child I was constantly being reminded to switch off that light, eat my dinner, or told, "We never had that during the Occupation". This is perhaps not really the kind of thing that a kid is interested in hearing. Although be to fair, I did arrive 15 years after my brother (OK, there was a war in between), and my parents were then in their 40s, so maybe I was an afterthought or a mistake. I'd like to think that my dad did try to say and do the right things in the years after my mum died. It cannot have been easy attempting to bring up a teenager on his own, especially one that was almost a stranger. And I would imagine that I did not help much myself. This probably goes a long way to explain why my father and I never really got on.

Much to my surprise there comes a time when you become responsible for your parents' well-being. It should be no great bombshell, but after years of having them care for you — often trying against the odds, and inevitably against your wishes, to keep you on a safe and steady course — to suddenly find them weak and frail comes as a shock.

I suppose that my dad's usual drunken antics, which spanned a period of 40 years, gave me a great start in caring for someone who was not always in control of their actions. It also brought home the very likely possibility that I would one day find him dead, which is what eventually happened.

The first real sign that this was a possibility occurred one morning, sometime in June 1994, a couple of months before our original French ride. I called in to drop my keys off at dad's — I would leave my car there while I was working at the bike shop. I found him, unable to move, on the sofa in the front room. Fortunately, I had brought Jane, my sister-in-law into town with me. As she was a trained state registered nurse, I asked her for help. It was fairly obvious that dad had had a stroke.

I gave his doctor a call, he came immediately, and confirmed what we suspected. He said that hospital was the best place for dad, called an ambulance and left. The ambulance arrived within 15 minutes. The paramedics put dad in a chair-like stretcher, covered him with a blanket, and took him to the hospital. I must say that he left the house like royalty, being carried aloft in that chair.

I went to the hospital to see him that evening, and I visited every night after work. Dad appeared to enjoy all the fuss and the regular meals (especially jelly and ice cream). This situation was new to me, and at times like these you don't look too far ahead. So it came as a bolt out of the blue when I was told that I would have to look after him when he came out of hospital in the very near future.

I imagine it was all standard practice for the social worker who imparted this information to me, and they did it all the time. But I found the way it was done was rather callous and abrupt. The message was either you take your father in, or we sell his house, take the money, and he goes to live in a state-run care home. I was taken aback by this but arranged a meeting with another social worker who I knew, and who explained the choices to me in a much a kinder way.

In July we visited my dad's lawyer. He explained that selling his house and giving the proceeds to the State was not the only option; we could sell his house and use the money to support dad in a private care home. We much preferred this option as neither Susan or I were bothered by any inheritance and we felt that this would provide him with better quality care.

So, with this in mind, we began a thorough and sometimes arduous inspection of nearly all the old folks' homes in Jersey. They ranged from the downright awful to places that were more like hotels. As it turned out, after a brief appraisal and proving he could fend for himself, dad was allowed to live independently back at home.

Dad received 'meals on wheels' for a short period, although the food that was delivered went in the bin. Despite their best efforts, dad was happier doing his own cooking. He didn't like to rely on people and was, at the very least, an individual and obstinate man. By the end of July he was back at home and often out and about. I know that because Matthew and I visited him on our way down to the boat for our first French trip in August 1994 but he was nowhere to be found.

Dad died the following year. But at 85 years old and having not really taken great care of himself for the best part of 30 years, he had a good innings. Having lost his wife and eldest son at a young age, I think it was only obduracy that kept him ticking.

With a long descent on the cards I decide to switch my dynamo back on. Knowing that we'd be heading uphill slowly today, I undid the generator this morning so that I didn't have to put up with the awful racket it makes. But now that we're going downhill it's a perfect opportunity to recoup some free power for my phone. I've been using the solar charger for putting some puff back in the Garmin, too, but on an overcast day like today I'm not expecting much success.

I swear that dynamo is cursed: as soon as I get it working a hill arrives. But it's only a temporary blip and we keep the speed quick and constant for a fair few miles. To our right we can see clouds at almost the same level as us, partially covering different parts of the valley. My attention, though, is on the other side of the road. I'm keeping my eye out for a turning to the left, towards our next waypoint: Bagnac sur Célé. I spot it and we dive down even further under trees.

Nothing lasts forever, though, and this moment of joy seems especially brief as we round a hairpin and face a climb out of a small valley. In the distance we can hear the constant chime of cowbells. It's like a 1980s hair-metal drummers' convention. I wonder if Christopher Walken is out there somewhere asking for more.

Music is something I've gone without on this trip. Because our power supply situation has been so parlous almost from the outset, I haven't taken advantage of the tunes stored on my phone. But I'm really missing it. In my life, music occupies very much the same kind of space as cycling, and my relationship with it is very similar. I can play a guitar a bit — I've been in various bands — but I wish I was better. Rather like my approach to cycling, I think music is a great thing to add joy to life, but I don't think it could be my entire life.

Music has also been a part of my journalism career, though. For six years or so I interviewed guitar players for *Guitar and Bass Magazine*. I've done some quite big names — Joe Perry from Aerosmith, Ace Frehley from Kiss, Phil Collen from Def Leppard, Joe Satriani, Dave Stewart, Richard Thompson. I'd love to have some stories about one of them being a real cocky arrogant berk but it's never happened, even when they've been under pressure. I interviewed Status Quo's Rick Parfitt on the phone at his home in Spain once. I could hear his twin babies causing him all sorts of grief in the background, but he was still a good sport. And it was nice for the shoe to be on the other foot for a change.

Much like pro cyclists, the famous guitar players I've dealt with seem to be appreciative of their luck. They don't have to have massive egos any more — they have nothing to prove. They're not boring. though. I once had a very restricted 15-minute interview with Mick Mars of Mötley Crüe who, for some reason, spent 12 of my precious minutes talking about hip replacements. I think he'd misheard a question.

As I mentioned, I tend to namedrop those musicians I've just interviewed on Twitter. But because most people think I only write about cycling, I regularly get asked: "Does so-and-so ride a bike, then?" (For the record, I ask every rock star I speak to if they cycle, just in case I can double up the story for two different magazine markets and get paid twice. Sadly, none of my guitarist interviewees has said yes.)

Playing the guitar for pleasure at home has much the same effect as going out for a bike ride. It calms me down and allows my brain to wander. Meanwhile, when I was in a band playing gigs, the effect of getting up on stage sparks much the same feeling of adrenaline — and then the same feeling of relief that you've survived — as riding a bike hard.

For all that climbing we've done so far today, I was expecting a fair bit more relief on the road away from Bagnac. The road is arrow straight but it's climbing slightly between quite pleasant open fields. It's a far cry from those rollercoaster carriageways of this trip's early days, but we've still got to turn our legs over. The slope gradually ramps up and it becomes a bit of a slog as it twists and turns in the shadow of the hilltop village at Montredon.

We reach a main road and follow it down towards the Lot Valley. It's a superb little descent — one of the few truly joyous moments on this trip so far. A small flight of swallows emerges from the hedge as we arrive and leads the way, playing and diving and swooping only a matter of feet in front of me. For a brief moment it's like being in a Disney movie.

Day 8 — More Cowbell

As we draw closer to Decazeville we go through a small place called Livinhac le Haut, which nestles in the curve of the River Lot and appears to be a popular stopping point for pilgrims on their way to Santiago de Compostela. I spot three of them looking at a large map board. I've always fancied having a crack at walking the route to Santiago, but Matt tells me outright I'll have to do it with Susan — he's not volunteering.

We have a breather on the northern side of the river and watch a number of pilgrims pass by with rucksacks on their backs, rough walking staffs in their hands and devotion in their eyes. My heart goes out to them. They come from all over the world and, unlike us, they hope for some level of enlightenment at the end of their journey. We hope for a hot shower, a soft bed and great food. Enlightenment can wait.

As we cross the bridge for Decazeville there's another family of pilgrims. You can tell they're obviously pilgrims because they're all carrying sticks. I can't help wondering if the Knights Templar now operate as a sort of de facto AA or RAC service for walkers doing this route? Do modern-day pilgrims have them on speed dial just in case they need them to save their asses?

We've both grown used to facing a final kick in the nuts each day on this ride but this is the one that leaves us metaphorically singing soprano. I knew it was going to be a tough climb after the bridge — it's got three little 'up' arrows on the map — but at 13 per cent it's borderline insane. We have to hop off and push, slowly passing a man and his son who have dismounted from their motorbike to pick berries at the roadside.

Even on what's already been a hard day, this is the hardest and by far the steepest thing we've faced. Last Sunday, when we started this 'jaunt' I really didn't fuss about hills. We knew we'd have to face some between Saint Malo and the Mediterranean. But now I'm starting to get in the habit of planning for them, avoiding them, and counting them down. Any climbs that appear unexpectedly, or which are bigger than I predict, I take very personally.

Eventually we reach the summit, although because this is an urbanised area it doesn't really deserve such a grand title. We simply reach the top of the hill.

We'll find a hotel here in Decazeville. Manda's already emailed me some addresses, but we figure we'll head into the town centre first and see if there's anywhere obvious we can stay.

That quickly proves to be a pointless idea — it's Sunday and c'est la France — so we have to retrace our steps a little and head up a side street. We find one of the establishments on our list. It looks far from busy but dad goes in and spends an inordinately long time trying to get things sorted while I guard the bikes. Finally we can unload all the bags and park the bikes in a little storeroom-come-kitchen round the side. 'Monsieur Traveltavern' at the desk says they'll be safe there, although he doesn't lock or even close the door as we leave. Where's dad's fastidious security consciousness now?

After that last mother of a hill, we finally see Decazeville lying beneath us. Last time we were here it was around midday, when all sensible folk hid indoors away from the blazing sun. This time we arrive at about 5pm but the place is equally dead.

Our plan is to find a hotel, charge up our devices and dry off our wet clothing from the previous day's rain. We find a hotel on the outskirts. It looks suitable and I go in to enquire about a room.

It seems like no-one is staying there; certainly all the pigeonholes behind 'mine host' have keys in them and there are only two cars in the car park, one of which belongs to the gentleman I'm dealing with now. Notwithstanding this, the proprietor takes a full five minutes to decide if there is space for us. He charges us a very reasonable 50€ for a twin room and helps us put our bikes away in what I think is an offshoot of the kitchen.

Our room is clean and comfortable. Unfortunately, though, all the plugs appear to be blocked off. Even the plug points in the hall outside have had the same treatment. This is a minor tragedy. Had we known, we might have picked somewhere else, or maybe even sought out a campsite.

Dad might say it's alright, but I reckon the hotel itself is a real dump, only a quarter star or so above Richie and Eddie's 'Guest House Paradiso'. The hallway lights are on push-button timers, so we have to sprint like two donkeys at the Derby from the dingy stairs to our room. The room is small and relatively unpleasant. It also seems that the first part of our grand plan — to charge our phones — looks unlikely to happen. All the plug sockets have been filled. At least we can definitely dry our clothes and dad has a small fight with the window to get it open. We hang, dangle and lay out every sodden thing we can.

I decide to go for a shower and by now we all know what else I'm going to do. But the shower is so small that as I bend over to cleanse that area which must be cleansed, I knock the hot tap, meaning that my red-raw arse gets a double whammy as a stream of boiling water scolds it. I say something rude.

I also notice my palms are starting to smell and peal. It's a bit of a worry, but nothing major: it happened after only a few days back in 1994. I'll just ride without wearing mitts for the rest of this trip.

After dad has his wash — as a good sport I warn him about the proximity of the shower's hot tap — we set off to find something to eat. There's a promising takeaway pizza place only a matter of yards from the hotel, but dad is already striding off at speed.

I don't know if all dads do this, but throughout my life I've known the old chap to get in these bizarre moods where he'll just walk, with no real direction or even goal in mind. Bearing in mind he has a very bad heel right now, I don't think it's the best idea but I dutifully follow him rather like a parent ruefully watching a stroppy urchin. Just as he's about to take us further uphill and away from the hotel, with absolutely no food outlets in sight, I suggest we should probably turn back. We can always have a drink at one of the two bars we've seen that are open.

That's good enough and we pop into a fly-ravaged tabac. Dad asks for a bottle of cider but the nice lady (I use the terms 'nice' and 'lady' relatively) has to disappear into a backroom to see what they've got. Unless you want a beer in a crappy little glass or a shot of Ricard, you're a troublemaker. Some cocky monsieur sitting at the bar — I can't decide if he's the bar lady's partner or just a regular loudmouth — starts haranguing us.

She comes back with a dust-covered bottle of cider. Dad reacts favourably and — after much debate between the woman and 'Monsieur Personality' in the corner — we're treated to a small tumbler of the stuff. Christ Almighty, I've just cycled 50 miles and climbed 3,000 feet, I need more than this.

Dad takes his time but I'm keen to hurry as a tramp we saw outside has come in, taken the stool next to me, and is chuckling in my ear. This is just about the worst experience yet on this trip. The guy stinks and I'd love to know what he is laughing about. Or perhaps I don't want to know.

The name Decazeville sounds like it should be an outpost in some far-flung corner of the French colonies, but it is actually a lot quieter than that. We don't see another soul in town during the hour or so that we walk around. Like the rest of France, Decazeville is shut.

Eventually we find a bar open, it has about four people in it: the barmaid; her daughter; the daughter's boyfriend; and a bloke who may be the proprietor. We're also joined by another chap who looks like he has not seen either a comb or soap for a year or two. He chuckles away to himself and capers about like a French Ben Gunn. I suspect that drink is the least of his addictions.

We ask for cider, which might just as well be fairy juice in these parts. The charming barmaid (it's actually been some time since she was a maid) manages to find a bottle of this extremely rare liquid and brings it out in triumph, wiping off the dust as she advances towards us. She also wisely cautions her daughter that I speak French. Sadly this warning did not reach the proprietor, who seems to find my conversation amusing. About as amusing as a pub with three customers and no cider. We finish the bottle of cider and strike out in the hope of food.

We march double time back to the pizza place, submit our order — the guy in there says it'll take 20 minutes — then go for a stroll in what I suppose should be called the suburbs. There is absolutely nobody around. Houses are shuttered and only a distant dog bark or rumble of traffic breaks the silence. Yet we're not out in the sticks, Decazeville is a fairly industrial conurbation. We return to the pizza place and sit at the counter.

The pizza is freshly made and looks superb, and the young guy behind the counter is friendly. We stock up on soft drinks and talk about our trip. He advises us that there will be some climbing tomorrow. No merde, Maigret.

Then it's back to 'Monsieur Rigsby's for the sprint betwixt stairwell and room door, and time to eat. The pizza is good and unlike on our first night, none of it is thrown away. We phone home and tell them our woes. Then it's time to plan tomorrow's route to Millau.

I see we'll be passing close to Balsac. Ha ha. That's cheered me up. I wonder if it's twinned with Nob End.

Day 8 — More Cowbell

RIDES OF PASSAGE

DAY 9

There Are Old Cyclists And There Are Bold Cyclists

**Monday August 22, 1994 — Marcillac to L'Hospitalet
(67.6 miles)
Monday August 10, 2015 — Decazeville to Millau
(69.7 miles)**

Matt aged 15

We started early and left the campsite by 7.30am. After going down a road that seemed to climb forever we reached the outskirts of Rodez. With careful map reading we managed to take shortcuts through a series of back lanes to the road we wanted for Millau.

After a while we got to a town called Agen. Here we bought four croissants, two apple turnovers and two peach custard slices. We ate all but the two croissants and headed on our way. After Agen, however, was a huge climb. At the top we had our last croissants and descended to Ségur.

In Ségur, Dad bought two cheese slices and two cans of Perrier, then we were almost attacked by three dogs. After 13km we got to the road that would take us to Millau. We descended quite a way on this and stopped near Bois du Four. Here, while sitting at the side of the road, a woman set her dogs on us. That made us move quickly.

It was a quick and easy descent to Millau but I ended up with a broken spoke and puncture, and subsequently strayed all over the road. I thought I was doing well just to keep control as the descent was so steep.

We entered Millau and Dad fixed my bike in a park/garden while I went to get food. I only managed to get some peaches, cheese, choccy, biccies, two cans of diet coke and some little cakes.

We left Millau at 3.30-4pm and started climbing towards the 'Causse du Larzac'. The climb went on for miles on an 'N' road, so we ended up pushing. By the time we got to the top we were both stuffed. We sat down and had the rest of the water and the peaches. One kilometre down the road we got to the Maison du Larzac, where Dad bought more water.

Still on the 'N' road, we got to La Cavalerie where we tried to buy a phone card (but did not succeed). We ate some of our little cakes and bought some wine for tea. By walking and riding, we got to l'Hospitalet and our camp for the night.

I set up the tent while Dad washed our clothes. We then had showers and tea: hot (very hot) Spanish sausage bought a couple of days ago, today's cheese, bread, white wine, small cakes, choccy biccies and water.

After tea we went to phone Mum but some bastard was in the phone box forever, so we didn't bother. We went back to camp and went to sleep.

Tomorrow we want to get up fairly early as it is a long day and we want to miss the traffic on the 'N' road we have to take.

Today we travelled 108.8km. Tomorrow we have to do the same if not more. LAST DAY TOMORROW HOORAY!!!!!!!!!

Arthur aged 42

The tent was damp again but we managed to set off around 07.30hrs. Matt struggled a bit early on. Quite Alpine here, cows have bells on. Managed to get on the right road from Rodez towards Millau.

Cake stop at Agen, croissants, apple puffs and peach Danish. Very old village with a drinking fountain in the middle. Steady riding onto Ségur — very southern France.

Bought pasty and water. Got to Millau reasonably fast. Matt had a puncture en route (slow one). Also another spoke broke. Set up a bike shop in an ancient monument and mended both. Sent Matt for food, he managed to get Coke and chocolate biscuits.

Mega climb out of Millau (went on for 7 kilometres) and very, very hot. We walked up, it took about an hour and a half. Stopped at the top to drink the warm coke and eat two peaches. Set off again and found a cafe further up the road. Bought four bottles of Vittell for £4(!) but at least they were cold.

Eventually made the campsite at around 18.30hrs, buying wine en route. Quite a good camp: nice setting and a bar/restaurant, but the bogs and showers are a bit crap if quite clean.

Tried to phone home but the phone was hogged by someone, so we went to bed.

Highlights of the day:
— Lady in wellington boots hosing down the toilets at Marcillac.
— Thunder rumbles regularly.
— Puncture (slow), could not find hole, so replaced tube.
— Another broken spoke.

Matt aged 36

I wake up in a bed for a change and it was a decent night's sleep by recent standards. Normally I can sleep through anything and no amount of daily concerns or impending worries keep me up, but on this trip I'm sleeping terribly. I thought all the exercise would have me exhausted — I certainly feel exhausted — but I think the lack of a pillow, along with a narrow sleeping mat and invariably a hard surface underneath has conspired to hamper my nightly journey to the land of nod.

I get up and go to the bathroom for my now well-practised morning routine. I'm shocked, and refreshingly it's not due to some unexpected dangleberry or sore-arse development. As I perch on the mighty throne I notice something scuttling about on the floor. It makes a big enough impact in the corner of my vision for me to initially think it could be a rodent. But then I get a good look as it emerges and strolls into the shower tray.

It looks like a 30-legged spider, with long, thin limbs and two huge antennae out the front. It must be a good three inches long. I've never seen anything like. It's almost the sort of thing a desperate has-been is forced to eat in *I'm A Celebrity...* I can't be fussed fighting and capturing it right now, I've got bigger fish to fry. But just as I'm hoping our multi-legged interloper will hang about long enough for me to show dad, it creeps under the doorway to the bedroom and disappears.

When I'm done abluting I ask dad if he saw it, but he says no. I'm not convinced. With his history on this trip I wouldn't be surprised if he'd actually had a chat to it, offended it, and it's decided to pitch up in a room over the corridor instead.

We haven't been able to literally recharge our batteries but at least all our clothes are dry. They're far from perfect, though: a lingering smell of sweat permeates all my gear. No matter. We dress, pack our pannier bags and head downstairs. 'Monsieur Richard Richard' isn't at his front desk, although there are two forlorn-looking couples enjoying his Continental breakfast. "Feeb, one boiled egg." But it's 8 o'clock, we need to get a shift on, and I suspect his high-security utility room may be open for us to retrieve our bikes.

I'm not wrong, it's probably been open all night. Thank goodness the bikes are still there — I think I mean 'thank goodness', although an extended session of cussing would have been just as apt — so we load up and set off.

Arthur aged 63

It's surprising how soft real beds feel when you have spent a week in a sleeping bag on a self-inflating mattress. We leave the hotel just after 08.00hrs. There is no sign of the manager who said that he would be there to help us retrieve our bikes. However, Matt goes in search and comes back with them.

Just as we load up, mine host appears to bid some other clients a very effusive farewell. I imagine that they must have had the 'petit déjeuner' and no devices that needed charging. Certainly they have the only other car in the hotel car park.

Leaving Decazeville is easy to begin with as there's a very helpful cycle path running alongside the ring road. But, with the kind of mileage we're doing, cycle paths tend to be momentary breaks from the reality of road riding, and soon we're back on a 'D' road heading towards our first big goal of the day: Rodez.

On the map last night it seemed this particular road looked quite substantial and we blast past a sign that I suspect says cyclists need to dismount or find another route in a couple of kilometres. I call forward to the old fella and ask him what he thinks the sign means, but he doesn't seem keen to pay any notice to it.

We make good time. It's obvious that this is a very busy main road. I have back-up route options in mind if need be, and soon it does become a need. Despite not showing up on Google Maps last night as I checked the route, this road becomes a dual carriageway — a big one — the type that meanders up a big hill, with other road bridges over it, and no real hard shoulder for us to hide on. That, coupled with the road sign earlier makes me think it's probably time to abandon this particular stretch of asphalt and find an alternative.

I call dad to stop just by a little slip road coming in from the right, so we can discuss options. I tell him my concerns.

"But it must be OK for us to ride here. Look, that's a cycle path," he says, pointing to a 100-yard stretch of gravel as the slip road merges into the main carriageway.

"That's a tiny bit of hard shoulder," I reply incredulously. "Where's the painting of a bike on the floor if it's a cycle lane?"

The old fella looks pretty annoyed. I can't decide whether it's because of my reaction to his foolish idea; the fact he realises it's a foolish idea; or just that he felt we were going well on this road and is loathe to break off on a slower side route. Throughout this trip his enthusiasm for getting places as quickly as possible hasn't waned. But, as I think we've established, I am far from a risk-taking hero.

The old man is not a stroppy kind of person. For all his talk about French heritage and his support for 'Les Bleus' on the rugby pitch, he actually has a very English sense of reserve and anger management. That is to say, he tends to hold it in until it bursts forth. I suppose the way it bursts forth can sometimes have a rather dramatic, Continental feel to it. But I can't ever remember him shouting or losing his temper with me or Ritchie.

If you were to ask us to remember a time when he'd lost his rag, Ritch and I would probably come up with the same story. It would be when he made a bit of a balls-up trying to parallel park one morning while dropping us off at school and ended up punching the steering wheel so hard it snapped down the middle. Not his finest moment, although most men with any spirit have done similar. And the fact that Ritch and I would both independently recall the same tragi-comedic episode shows, I think, that he's been pretty steady.

Another moment I remember was when we went to see our first ever gig a few years after our 1994 French ride. My grandfather died in 1995 and with some of the inheritance dad decided to take Ritchie and me to see our two favourite rock bands, Kiss and Ozzy Osbourne, at the 1996 Monsters of Rock festival in Donington. For two kids from Jersey it was like a dream. We had a chauffeur pick us up from Birmingham Airport and transport us to the Donington Manor Hotel, where Barry Sheene used to stay in his racing days. The memory of that weekend is the reason I'm keen to take my boys to see any and every event we can (in fact, I took them to see Kiss at Donington just a few weeks before this bike ride).

Obviously the memory of seeing the fireworks, and the Kiss helicopter, and the sheer spectacle of a concert that size is what remains most prominent in my mind. But one other thing sticks there, too. The night before the show we'd strolled from our hotel in Castle Donington to a nearby chippy. There was a drunk ne'erdowell in there with his mate. I remember the mate was trying to keep him under control, but the guy was being a true arsehole and he started abusing dad.

Having lived in the UK for half my life, I'm now aware that you tend to encounter these kinds of losers, especially when they're bored by village life out in the sticks. But back then we were two kids and their dad from a small island in the Channel, and England was a little bit threatening.

Dad just ignored the bloke and we went back to the hotel. When you're 17, as I was then, with anger and hormones flowing through your body, you're secretly hoping your dad is going to morph into the Incredible Hulk and teach this scumbag a lesson. But dad's reaction actually taught me something very important: pick your battles. In this case, arguing or chinning some drunk, gobby kid in an East Midlands backwater is not a fight worth starting, no matter how much he momentarily offends your pride.

We continue to follow our route, which seems to favour motorways — in fairness, our route directions are about 20 years out of date — but soon get tired of big roads and cut off cross country while we still can. Matt does some brilliant map reading and we reach Marcillac Vallon in time for some breakfast. This must be an ultra-upmarket town because it not only has public toilets but the dogs are on leads, too.

I leave dad to play with his camera while I go to do breakfast duties. Dad has run out of wet wipes — not surprising really, considering he seems keen to wipe down everything he can get his hands on — so a supermarket would be handy. I can't find one of those but there's a boulangerie just a matter of yards away. The lady inside is initially very pleasant, but I realise I'm forgetting to say "s'il vous plaît", and she's already started to bridle. Hey ho. But it reminds me that the language barrier works both ways and perhaps I shouldn't be so quick to judge.

Dad and I sit on a bench under a little boulevard of trees at the side of the main road and eat our croissants. There are some municipal workers out today and they're tidying up the leaves that have fallen onto the sandy, gritty pavement. It's a welcome breather for us, we've been going fairly well. A road sign says Rodez is only 20 kilometres; the map suggests it'll be tough going, though.

The route out of Marcillac is fairly busy. Not constant traffic like the 'D' road we left after Decazeville, but it's far from being a country lane. And it does indeed start to climb; fairly gradually at first, then steeper and higher as it weaves around the side of the valley. We pass through Salles la Source, a pretty little village perched on the side of the cliff, and take photos of the old-fashioned houses all around. The road keeps going up but, unlike yesterday, there's no pushing and walking involved, this is all eminently rideable but we do need frequent stops to rest our legs and have a drink. We're getting through serious amounts of water today, despite the temperature only being in the mid-20s — fairly cool compared to some days on this trip.

We ride partly under tree cover, partly with the valley open to our side. A plump, mature roadie speeds down the hill in the opposite direction to us and calls out that the summit isn't far away. We don't take his word for it and prepare for a lot more grovelling, but he's quite right. Eventually the road plateaus and it becomes clear that we're entering the suburbs of Rodez. Soon there's even a segregated cycle lane, although I opt to keep us on the road as it'll make navigation a trifle easier.

We press on, meeting three fellow cyclo-tourists who are coming in the opposite direction. From memory, there were very few cyclo-tourists in 1994, and there's not many more in 2015. Do they take a different route or is

France just not that exciting? What we do see is a group of American riders descending past us. Judging by their clothes and the lack of luggage on their bikes, I guess they are either on an escorted trip that carries your kit or they are having a holiday in the area.

We don't have to venture too far into Rodez. The route I've planned for us will skirt around the town to the north-east and it's not actually as tricky or as busy as I imagined. There's a good flow of cars around, and any city's road signs are confusing to people who aren't initiated with them. But we find our way quite easily and join the right road, parallel to the train track.

Considering France is seen as being such a cycling-keen country, we've spotted precious few bike shops. However, Rodez makes up for that with four cycle shops in the space of just a few miles, interspersed among other retail and industrial outlets. Having avoided Brive so thoroughly a few days ago, this is just about the most urban or developed part of our route so far.

The sun has come out again and we reach a roundabout that joins onto an official 'N' road, normally something we wouldn't touch with a barge pole. I also spot a sign that says Millau is 73 kilometres away. I know we only need to ride on the 'N' road for about 50 yards, so that's no problem. But the sign has rattled me slightly — by my reckoning Millau should only be 60km away. But we must never forget, c'est la France, so don't panic.

We turn right onto the D29. It's a decent little stretch guiding us along a wide open valley floor. The first village we come across is Agen d'Aveyron. We um and ah momentarily about stopping for supplies, but against type it is dad who wisely suggests we stock up — we are very low on water and food. Whether it's the heat or tiredness, we seem to be making more rudimentary errors as we go further on this trip and manage to ride right past the village shop, needlessly taking on a short climb towards the church. It's only as we retrace our tyre treads, cursing that this damn place doesn't have anywhere to buy food, that we spot the mini-mart.

Dad heads in and comes out with cheese, two tins of salad nicoise, Orangina, water, biscuits, bread and an old woman. It's the 'matron de mini-marché' who has sportingly helped him carry his purchases. We sit and eat (dad and me, not the old lady shopkeeper). It's getting hot again, so sun spray goes on. We're now down to our bottle of factor 20, the factor 30 having run out a day or two ago.

At Agen d'Aveyron we pull off the road and go in search of food just in time to hear the church sound 65 o'clock. Despite a little confusion, a splendid lunch of bread and cheese ensues.

162

We take the chance to call home and Matt chats to his boys. Nowadays, Susan and I are called the 'elderlies' by Matt's twins. (Crikey, I remember when I thought that 25 was elderly, and for an elderly, that's good remembering.) What the boys mean is that we are, in fact, grandparents. This is an interesting situation: you don't have responsibility for their upbringing — at least we don't — but you'd like to share some of your accumulated wisdom with them. At present they are too small to have much interest, and who can blame them? But perhaps there is a special niche there for grandparents.

Of course, being a grandparent is also the official sign you are getting old, which in this day and age seems to be the ultimate disgrace. What's so infuriating is that it creeps up on you without you noticing. One moment you are vibrant, full of energy and sharp as a pin; the next you are worn out, sleepy and forgetful. It generally all goes wrong in unison. Your body heads south, like the swallows in winter. The muscles you may or may not have had disappear. And a complete stranger invades your wardrobe mirror.

I used to embrace the male menopause. I thought it was great fun to suddenly be interested in motorbikes, loud shirts and impressing younger women again. Although in fairness, I think that most men have those interests at any age. I seem to have had the problem for about 20 years, so it's now getting both embarrassing and boring, even to me. How my immediate family are coping, I can only imagine. I do try to grow old gracefully but it's not much fun. Fortunately the world cannot see your sagging chest, waistline and neck if you are fully clothed.

So what else happens? Well, baldness is quite common. I started to go bald when I got married at 24, but please don't think that hair loss is a by-product of marriage. Having had this happen to me at a relatively young age it was something I had got used to, and like many men sported a pelmet of hair surrounding my head. For the past 20 years I have taken to shaving my head completely. Not only does it not give away my age, but it's a very tidy look that is easy to maintain.

Eyesight is another thing that begins to fail as you get older. Again, I'm quite fortunate here (if you can call it that): I have been wearing glasses since I was seven. According to my father, my short-sightedness was caused by sitting too close to the television as a small boy. In fact, the telly was as big as a phone box but had a screen the size of a box of Milk Tray, so it's no surprise that I sat close. Another point of interest with aging spectacle wearers is that you can pinpoint when they purchased their spectacles with some certainty because styles change. For example, those elderlies with two giant screens on their faces probably bought their glasses in the 1970s. That theory won't work for me, though, I'm well trendy!

Grey hair is another giveaway. Many people, including many men, dye their hair. Dyed hair looks great on the young, but pathetic on the old. And it's very obvious, so why bother? This may go some way to explaining why I sport a grey beard. I would be up for dying it, but not a colour that could be my own. I would like red, blue or purple to show what a wacky character I am, or maybe that I really don't give a toot.

Did I mention teeth? Probably not, I'm getting on a bit. Again, I am lucky as I think I have quite good teeth, not helped at all by the school dentist, who seemed to be paid by the filling. Nowadays I have a brilliant dentist who keeps my pearly whites in good order, but then I am a bit vain. Somewhat along the lines of the thrifty glasses wearers are those who shun the idea of replacing a missing front tooth with a plastic one. Every time they smile it looks like London after the Blitz.

Here are some other signs of old age to look out for: double-checking that you've done things, such as locking the front door; wearing comfy clothing such as fleeces, baggy trousers and trainers (I don't); being obsessed with buses, bus stops and bus timetables; complaining a lot; and jumping queues but acting innocently afterwards. And here is an extra one for men: do you still fancy older women? When your Mrs Robinson moment is over, you are officially an elderly.

Although Susan keeps telling me that I am not old, I'm not certain that she's right. That said, as all us elderlies know, it is only the people who are 20 years older than us who actually are ancient.

For some reason we've found the ride after lunch something of a challenge every day this trip. First of all, we're both experiencing incredible amounts of lactic acid in our legs. It feels almost like the stuff is collecting in great jerry cans under our skin, weighing down every pedal stroke. And for me, after every off-bike moment there's still that gradual lowering onto the saddle process that needs to be followed, which is made all the more difficult with heavy legs. Inside my head, certainly since day three, I've been saying to myself: 'I can't go on, I can't go on.' It's not the positive mental attitude we're supposed to adopt in moments of difficulty. But I'm still here, and we're getting ever closer to the Mediterranean.

I'm also finding reasonable success in a pain-coping technique I've used before. In moments of sharp discomfort, I've noticed pain comes in waves. Hit your nail with a hammer and you'll feel the initial shock, then a very momentary lull before the real lasting pain kicks. I'm getting a similar thing every time I get on the saddle. But by focusing on the lull, the period where the pain hasn't truly hit home, it's helping to just take the edge off things.

Our route may now be among different scenery, but in terms of the gradient we face, this afternoon isn't far different to this morning. After Agen the road ramps upwards. There are some desperately steep moments that require a drink stop midway, but it's largely a constant climb that just becomes a tad tougher as we near the summit. For the first time on this trip, though, we're rewarded with the knowledge we've climbed a genuine, classified 'col'. A road sign says this is the Col d'Aujol at 870m, getting on for 3,000ft.

We're both feeling a bit wobbly at the top, but there's a strange, relaxed elation, too. Just to make the moment even more significant a magnificent, immense metal statue marks the summit. It was only put up this year and it's the local area's answer to Tyneside's 'Angel of the North'. We could stay at the side of the road and look at the view of this great creation from a distance, but we decide to go up the farm track to the statue's base. I once did a ride through the Scottish Borders for an article and saw the signs for the William Wallace statue that looks out over the River Tweed at Bemersyde. But I was wearing road shoe cleats that were hard to walk in and didn't bother going to see it. I've slightly regretted it ever since.

From up here the view is incredible. To the right we can see heavy, dark clouds over a fulsome farm of wind turbines, but it's so far away we don't have anything to worry about. To our left there are the sharp lines of the Massif Centrale, way away in the distance. Other interesting sights are closer to home. I spot the wheels from a child's Lego set on the floor. Up this path, so far removed from signs of any nearby civilisation, I can't help but laugh. Surely this is some cosmic joke to see if I've overcome my emotional collapse of a few days earlier.

I look at the map. We're essentially on a plateau of sorts and in 15 miles or so we'll reach the other side of it, as it joins the big 'D' road towards Millau. That point is at exactly the same height as we're at here, yet I can see the road instantly drops down, quite significantly. Dammit, we're going to be losing height.

It's all good fun as we crack on, but there's no great joy in the prospect we'll have to recover all this altitude. We level out after a few miles and stop in the little enclave of Ségur. It's about as far removed from the picture postcard Ségur le Château of a few days ago as you could find — this is simply a roadside village with nothing more to recommend it than a small supermarket.

Matt and I press on. The soil is now red, so we know we are in the south of France. We stop at a shop in Ségur to purchase what we were told is the only bottle of cider for miles around. While Matt is in the store I wait outside and am shouted at by a Jack Russell terrier (or should that be a 'Jacques' Russell terrier?). I remember this area being a bit fruity for dog incidents back in 1994. I wonder why that is.

There's a tough but short climb out of Ségur, but that's really the only noticeable hardship and we're soon on the 'D' road to Millau. Reality and the map don't tally, but for once it's in our favour. I can't understand how we haven't lost significant height since the top of the Col d'Aujol because it feels as if we've been riding downhill a lot. But I'm not knocking it. Sadly the joy is short lived and the D911 is as much of a risk as its name suggests. Huge articulated lorries blast past from the minute we join it.

I've been a bit hard on certain aspect of French life this trip but it would be unfair not to praise French drivers for the way they overtake cyclists. True, their driving generally might be near the knuckle — we've regularly seen cars tailgating each other at quite astronomical speeds — but when it comes to giving us room, I've felt a great deal safer here than in either the UK or Jersey. I once spoke to an ex-pat Frenchman about why French drivers seem to drive so recklessly among each other. He said it was because they know where the extremities of their cars are better than English people. He didn't mention whether they know the limits of their braking performance, tyre grip and road surface, though.

I'm as guilty as anyone when it comes to rampant generalisations, but I do find there are some particular motoring groups that tend to offer the most danger.

The first involves German cars and this can be further divided by brand. We'll leave out Porsche as I don't have any strong feelings about them. The worst are obviously BMW drivers, who need to get where they're going as quickly as they can, the roads were built for them, and whether you're a cyclist or another car driver you're an obstacle that really should disappear as they approach because they are very important people.

Some Mercedes drivers offer many of the same characteristics but there's also an interesting sub-group who are completely oblivious to where the corners of their car are. So, if it's any consolation, the old gentleman in that massive E-Class estate wasn't trying to kill you, he simply didn't know his nearside front wing was so close to the pavement. Meanwhile, Audi drivers can range anywhere from normal to über-obnoxious, although you tend to remember the worst ones most.

Then there are Volkswagen drivers. Historically you'd expect VWs to be driven by relatively unassuming people, but modern VWs seem to exude an air of superiority that's not far short of their posher Germanic siblings. VW Golfs and especially the hot, quick versions can be particularly aggressive.

Minis — effectively junior BMWs — can be a handful too. And for all German brands there's one final factor: the bigger the car, the more likely the driver will be 'unhelpful'.

Add to this list people carriers of any description driven by unfulfilled middle-aged men. Ten-year-old saloons driven by ruffians. Mini-cabs, taxis and buses. Big SUVs driven by mums late for the school run. And white van drivers. Frankly, I wouldn't let most people loose with a shopmobility scooter, far less tonnes of motorised metal. Because of that, I'm really not keen on this big road, so at the next junction we opt to head down towards a village called Saint Leons.

Before beginning our descent into Millau, we head into a very pretty wooded area with a deep valley on one side. I notice that the sweet chestnuts and elderberries are already ripe, a month or two before ours back home.

If I've been hard on the French, I've been equally hard on French roads on this trip. The truth is, a lot of the routes we've followed have either been too exhausting or too busy to enjoy. Here, deep among greenery, with pretty little houses dotted between the trees on the hillsides, I feel we're somewhere truly special. There's a surreal element to it all, especially as we spot little boards interspersed along the side of the road explaining the local flora and fauna. We reach the village centre and read a board that explains there's a nearby museum called Micropolis — 'La Cité Des Insectes' — which is dedicated to entomologist Jean-Henri Fabre.

Dad has to climb off and push as we head away from Saint Leons. I can just about keep spinning but it's a surprisingly hard slog through country lanes. We spot a sign that warns of a stop line in '5 kilometres'. There's nothing like being prepared.

Eventually we rejoin the fearsome D911 as it heads south on the last section to Millau. And it's the traditional kick in the goolies. Not only is it longer than we thought, we also face the re-emergence of our old friend: the straight, rolling, rollercoaster 'D' road. Eventually we reach a point where the 'D' road joins the motorway to continue over the Norman Foster-designed, awesome 1,000ft-high Viaduc du Millau.

Now here's another funny thing about the old chap. When we were plotting and planning this trip, he said: "The good thing is, they've got this big bridge so we won't even have to drop into and climb out of Millau this time." Then, when I looked into it and discovered it's a motorway— so definitely not something we'd be able to use while riding bicycles — he was a bit disappointed. Yet I can remember him not being particularly keen to abseil off a 40ft tower, so I dread to think how he would have reacted to being up a 1,000ft viaduct. In any case, there's no way on earth you'd get me on that thing riding a bicycle.

We can see Millau nestled way, way down below with huge hills all around it, so we follow smaller roads through a fairly barren hinterland, pockmarked by only a few industrial or commercial units. Soon we're dropping around the edge of this natural bowl, then right in among the houses on the upper slopes of Millau. This area is a particularly strange place, part San Francisco, part Brazilian favelas. It's certainly not a descent I can enjoy.

We have a fantastic view of the celebrated suspension bridge that allows traffic to bypass the valley. Matt tells me it's not for cyclists, though.

Then we take to narrow back roads to bring us into Millau. It takes us through the suburbs, past small bungalows with busy gardens and ugly apartment blocks. I thought it was a bit more attractive on our last visit, but on that occasion we really only passed through quite quickly, not withstanding the half hour or so I spent mending a puncture in the 'pop up' workshop that I created in what I think was an early Roman site of historic importance.

This time we plan to stop in Millau overnight, so we dismount in the busy streets and walk in the direction of 'le Camping'. We find this near the River Tarn.

We reach Millau centre ville. It seems there are a fair few campsites hereabouts and they're all down by the river. The town is absolutely buzzing with cars and people. However, after spending nine days in sleepy France I find it all a little bit overwhelming.

With a bit of navigating we reach the right area and it's obvious this is nothing like anywhere we've been yet on this journey. There are people canoeing and kayaking, there are paragliders overhead, and there are young folk everywhere. 'Where are all the young people in France?' we've been asking each day on this trip. The answer seems to be: Millau.

We cross a bridge over the river, hop off the road and head through a pedestrian underpass to the first campsite office we find. It looks OK, if a little bit seedy with people smoking and lounging about on plastic chairs outside the front. Dad heads in to sign us up and — good news — the lady has agreed to recharge my power bank. I'm quite proud that he's taken the initiative to sort this out.

But pride is a difficult bedfellow who never lingers long. Dad comes out and says we've got the last pitch in the campsite, although unfortunately it's right next to the toilets. Last pitch in the place, eh? Where have I heard that one before? OK, I don't care about being near the loos, that's fine. I ask the old chap how we get in. He's not sure, but he points the way back down the underpass to the other side of the road. Really? I can sense the people on their plastic chairs looking at us. They look at us even more bemusedly as I follow dad in completely the opposite direction from where we've just paid. Is he sure this is the right way? He sets off round the bend — as in, he rides round a corner, not he's gone mental, but it's a close call — and returns in a minute or two to say, no it must be back where we paid. Unbelievable. (For the record, I am not making this up: we genuinely did pay to camp at a campsite office, then turn round, cross to the other side of the road and head in the opposite direction to another completely different campsite.)

Millau is very busy because it is also a water sport centre, but we are lucky again because we manage to secure the last pitch in the site, opposite 'les sanitaires'. This pitch is destined to be for tents because there is no way you'd fit anything else on it. Most of our fellow campers are installed in caravans or camping cars, and are playing boules as if their lives depend on it.

Matt feels that the place is rather seedy, I have to agree but it is not horrendously expensive and the kind woman at reception puts our power bank on charge. I like the way the site is closed off by a locked gate in the evenings, although you wouldn't have to be Raffles to get through the smaller garden gate to the outside world that happens to be adjacent to our pitch.

Sure enough we find the gates into the campsite — would you believe it, just a few feet from the campsite reception — and our pitch is as described.

"That's right, she said it was next to the toilets," dad says loudly as he points to somebody's static home.

"I think those are the toilets there actually, dad," I say, gesturing towards the double glazed room clearly containing rows of cubicles, rather than somebody's pride and joy holiday residence.

Our pitch isn't much to write home about. In fact, it looks suspiciously like the kind of area you'd use to store big commercial dustbins. The rest of the campsite is relatively unpleasant, too, with fat 30 or 40-year-old geezers playing boules. I'm sure I saw one look over and gesture towards us in much the same way you'd see established prisoners greet the new pretty boys in a jailhouse movie. At best, the site has the feel of being a 'lad's weekend away' kind of place.

We put up the tent, fighting a losing battle with the rock-hard earth below, and I offer to head back over the bridge to Millau's centre ville to see if I can find supplies. I decide to walk rather than ride.

Away from the river it seems like a fairly normal Continental town, with the kind of streets you'd find anywhere from Paris to Lyon. I spot a mini-mart and log its place in my memory in case I can't find anything further on. There's another shop with roast chicken hanging outside, and then I reach the central square, which seems to be undergoing a lot of building work. The area is heaving with bars and cafes and shops and people. In certain conditions — ie, if we were staying in a hotel having driven here — it looks like quite a fun town, but I can't really stand exploring much more right now.

I head back to the mini-mart and buy crisps, chocolate, drinks, biscuits and a Toffee Crisp to enjoy on the return walk to camp. Together, my purchases could hardly be called a feast, but they'll do. There's a nice girl serving, although she gets the hump when I bring out my 50 euro note. It's a big one my dear, I hope you can deal with it. As it happens, she can't, and needs to delve into her own furry purse for enough change.

Matt arrives back from the shops and has brought another banquet of sorts. I also notice he has put a Toffee Crisp wrapper in our rubbish. Where's my Toffee Crisp, I wonder.

The old chap has got things organised at camp and we're set fair for the evening. Of course, certain personal issues need attending to, so that's done and I have a wash. It's only now that I realise I must have forgotten my magic towel at the hotel this morning — dammit! It's worth about as much as the entire furnishings of the room it's been left in. Still, it'll be a perfect size for 'Monsieur Centipede'.

Dad and I sit down to eat dinner but I can sense something's wrong. I think it's the reemergence of 'Captain Paranoia'. The old chap has put his bags on the outside of the tent, resting against the tent porch. We can see them under the gap between earth and rip-stop material — in real terms they're no more than a foot away — but he can't see *all* of them. In his head, I think I know what's happening: 'Somebody could levitate nearby, silently open my bag flaps without us noticing, and then steal something of immense value from within.'

He can take the stress no more and gets up to move the bags inside the tent porch. In the process he kicks over our open bottle of cider. Damn those imaginary French robbers for dealing us this blow once again.

It inspires a bizarre conversation. "I'm sure on the last trip we went out around the towns we stayed in more," I say. "Like we did last night."

"Yes, well last night was OK for us to both go round that town because at least there was some security," dad replies, almost seeming to suggest we took a bit of a chance heading out in Decazeville.

"Security?" I say. "What do you mean? We were in a hotel!"

"Yes, that's what they call it, a hotel," he says indignantly.

Don't worry if this conversation makes no sense to you; it makes no sense to me either.

In theory, tomorrow could be our last day, but as I look at the map it'll be a hell of a ride to cover the 80 miles to Sète in one go. The biggest problem we face is getting from down here in Millau up the overbearing cliff that currently has us in its shadow. It's roughly 1,200 feet of climbing in about three and a half miles. I think I've found a sneaky route away from the main road but we won't know how possible it is until we try it. Meanwhile, even once we get to the top of the hill there's a problem in the shape of a huge dual carriageway, which we might not be allowed to ride on.

For the first time on this trip, I'm truly nervous as I go to sleep. Tomorrow it could be make or break for us in terms of all three areas of concern: route, danger and fitness.

RIDES OF PASSAGE

DAY 10
Death Or Glory

**Tuesday August 23, 1994 — L'Hospitalet to Sète
(59.5 miles)
Tuesday August 11, 2015 — Millau to Gignac (51.4 miles)**

Matt aged 15

I woke up at 7am but Dad got up at 4.30am. He couldn't get to sleep and had heard thunder, so he brought in some of the washing. By the time I woke, a storm was quite near and the taking down of the tent was delayed for five or ten minutes.

We left the camp on an 'N' road, which we followed for miles going up and down. Eventually, after about 20km, we reached a massive descent. This took us through a huge tunnel and we even had to stop as our wheel rims were getting so hot that they might burn the tyres.

We reached Lodève where Dad bought two whirly cakes and two raspberry shortcakes. We found a phone box and rang Mum to say we were alright, then got back on the road for a further 21km until Clermont l'Hérault. Here we went to a supermarket and bought two bottles of water, two bottles of flavoured fizzy water, one carton of orange juice and one big bottle of Oasis orange squash.

We left this town and finally got off the 'N' road.

Eventually we saw Sète, a huge rock in the middle of the sea. On the way there we passed a long line of factories and arrived in the town near its train station. Then we tried to find a campsite by asking people. Most interesting were two old boys sitting on a bench. A woman in a boulangerie, who thought Dad was from Marseille, told us the camp was 15km away.

That was too far for our liking so we went looking for a hotel. The first one we tried, recommended to us by one of the old boys, was full up so Dad went to a post office and I watched the boats jousting on the canals.

We eventually came upon the 'Grand Hotel Sète', which would take us. After parking our bikes in a really modern car park, we went into our room. Dad did a load of washing while I watched TV. We phoned Mum from our room and then had baths!!

After that we went out to a little Italian restaurant. I had salad with smoked ham and blue cheese, then cheese, tomato, egg and smoked ham pizza. Dad had salad niçoise and then spaghetti.

We came back to our room, did some washing and wrote our journals. Dad quickly rang Mum again and we went to sleep at about midnight.

In total we have travelled 95.7km today.

DURING THE WHOLE TRIP WE HAVE COVERED 1,003KM!

Arthur aged 42

Hooray — last leg. Quite worried about the use of 'N' roads but much of it has a separate cycle lane. Made good progress along good downhill tarmac.

It rained last night (thunder and lightning), so I got sprayed by Matt. Also, the clean and, as usual, wet washing got filthy again as we rode. Went through a new tunnel at Pas de L'Escalet — we walked with rear lights flashing.

Cake stop at Lodève and phoned Susan. Only five units on our card left, so it had to be a very quick chat. Moderately horrendous 'N' road after the descent and Lodève. Could smell the aniseed in the air. Decided to walk after turning right into Clermont l'Herault.

Matt discovered a quick route to Sète avoiding more 'N' roads. We fuelled up with water and fruit juice at Clermont L'Herault. The road to Sète took forever and was very bumpy and rough.

Seemed like miles to go along 'N'-type roads, even when we could see Sète. Stopped near train station so went in to ask about going to Avignon with bikes. It's possible twice a day.

Then tried to find a campsite. Different advice meant we decided on a hotel and luxury this evening. The Grand Hotel was our choice. Not cheap, but life is short. Went out to eat, full after only two courses.

Highlights of the day:
— Fast roads, downhill and smooth.
— Went through tunnel.
— Long descents — wheels too hot to touch.
— Secret code to get into hotel garage.
— Dined out — Sète humming with people.
— Dried washing properly for the first time on hotel balcony. Carefully pinned so that it would not fall three floors down.
— Phoned Sue twice from hotel.

Matt aged 36

So, our last day — or is it? I have a strong suspicion we won't be able to quite reach Sète today. For the last day or two I have been trying to prime dad to accept that this tour might take us 11 days rather than 10 — I'm not sure he's quite coming round to the idea. If the weather forecast is to be believed, it's going to be über hot and we've got a whole host of potential problems route-wise to overcome. I plotted our course until late last night but I'm not sure how lots of it is going to work out — there are many unknowns ahead.

We get up early for the big day and I see to those things that need to be seen to. I'm still putting cotton wool in the sore crevice between my thigh and groin, but I've reduced the cushioning from two pads to one. It's getting better — that nice girl at the pharmacy in Larches knew what she was talking about.

By 7.30am we're ready to roll. One of the charming quirks of French campsites is that they lock you in at night and the main gates aren't yet open. Dad and I have to join forces to hoik our bikes up the stairs and through a small pedestrian gate.

Arthur aged 63

Despite the high mileage that we cycled yesterday, I had difficulty getting back to sleep after hearing several loud bangs going off in the dark last night. One was very, very close, and sounded not unlike a pistol going off. Matt slept like a log throughout the night, though, and he now thinks that I have an overactive imagination.

It wasn't the only thing I heard last night. Right next to our tent stands a lovely camping car with a small separate tent a few feet away. In the early morning, with the steady roar of a snorer echoing around the campsite, I realised why someone had been banished to sleep outside on their own.

We leave Millau and follow the main road out, over the bridge and uphill for only a short distance before finding the start of our secret route just beyond a service station. Back in 1994 we spent almost two hours walking up the main hill that took us out of the town. Under the baking sun and with cars racing past us, it was not pleasant. This time, thanks to the miracle of the iPhone, Matt thinks he has discovered another road that runs up the hillside but which is not a main thoroughfare.

The first back road we need begins just behind a McDonalds and takes us past a few houses on the climb's lower slopes. We're going well until we turn a corner and face a supremely steep concrete ramp that leads up to the 'D' road we are trying to avoid. I knew we'd have to join the big road for a very short section, but I didn't expect the trail to it to be this unhelpful. It's not quite a sheer wall, but with bikes weighing six stone each, it's hard to negotiate.

Through team work and a whole lot of luck we pop out onto the main road and follow it for 50 yards or so as it curves around a large hairpin bend. Then we branch off right onto a small road called Montée Royale — a very James Bond-ish name for something that is effectively a fire track — and can relax. Phew, that's the first worry answered and overcome.

It's steep and we've got to go a long way up, but at least we're away from the traffic. We stop every now and then to take a photo of Millau slowly shrinking beneath us. I also break out the last of the cheap chocolate energy bars I've been keeping in case of emergency. From time to time dad is happy to spin on in a low gear, but I'm sticking to pushing and trying to find shade where I can. Already at 9am it's very, very hot.

As we climb, Millau grows smaller by the minute until it resembles a trainset way below us. We can see the river, the bridges, the apartments and the road that we escaped on. From our vantage point we can also see right across the valley that Millau lies in, with the 'puys' — the ancient dormant volcanoes that litter the landscape — and of course more wind farms in the distance.

On the side of the road are signs for the GR71D walking route. The country is criss-crossed with GR routes, these are called 'Sentiers de Grand Randonnées' which are long distance footpaths that go across France, and indeed many other European countries. They are ideal if you've got lots of time and don't mind being completely away from it all. It appears that the 71D is a six-day walk around the area which heads for Larzac. It must be a very wobbly route, we plan to be there within an hour or two. Beside the GR signs are marked mountain bike routes. Again, it's all very civilised and perfect if you have enough time (and a mountain bike).

This little road we're following doesn't just zigzag, each section is almost parallel to the one before, but it's a fairly pleasant experience. Eventually the slope levels out just enough for us to hop back in the saddle and start riding again properly. After more photos at the top we emerge onto the plateau of the Causse du Larzac, which is nothing short of a desert landscape. It's barren, and open, and desolate.

We ride away from the summit along a crazy rock-strewn stone path and it's quite clear we have no choice but to hop onto the dual carriageway that runs alongside. We push our bikes up to the road and cycle on the hard shoulder next to the Armco barrier. The traffic gives us plenty of room but I've seen the speed limit sign — 110kph (70mph) — and when you've got vehicles blasting past at that kind of velocity, even a good 10 feet away, it tends to sharpen the senses. I'm eager to get off this as quickly as possible but the old chap is feeling the heat a fair bit and is having trouble keeping up.

As the time seems appropriate, let's talk a little about death. As a fully-fledged hypochondriac it's something I think about a lot and today is the day where I am most fearful of meeting my maker. First of all, there was that climb — if that didn't give me a heart attack, I know nothing will. Now there is this very fast, potentially very dangerous dual carriageway we need to follow for a short while.

And if we're thinking about death, I suppose we'd better think about God. Don't worry, I'm not a born-again type who's about to start preaching. Apart from anything else, I don't find that attitude very British. Having said that, I personally find it hard to imagine the magic of the world we see around us — even somewhere as bleak as the landscape we're currently crossing — has come about through happenstance rather than some element of design. I believe the fact we all have a conscience and the ability to think is a sign that there's something beyond what we can see and hear and touch.

I admit I am concerned that when I finally shuffle off this mortal coil there will be a point where I'm judged. I hope we'll all be allowed into the next place, we'll just be given a talking to about where we went wrong. Like most people, I've spent some time wondering just why we're here and what we're here to do. The best answer I can come up with is to try to leave the world in a slightly better shape than we arrived. That doesn't have to be in a save-the-planet global sense. I think we've just got to try to leave our little corner of reality no worse than when we were born.

That's why I believe the way people look after their children is so important. Even if you are a great artist, writer, engineer or politician, there's no guarantee your professional or creative legacy will remain to any great extent. But the effect that your children, and their children, and their children, and every subsequent descendant has on the world is immeasurable. So probably best to not knacker them up.

Because of this — unlike many cycling journalists and cyclists generally — I don't actually want people riding bikes all the time. Any higher power who has decided to purposely put us here must have bigger goals in mind than to just spend our lives spinning our legs.

I once had a mid-dinner argument with a good friend of mine who was spouting grandiose proclamations about the significance of pro bike racing. I remember him saying: "But pro cycle racing is a metaphor for life." Others round the table — all bike journalists — nodded sagely.

I said that was nonsense.

I have never seen anything in pro cycle racing that comes close to the joy and stress of marriage, or birth, or any of the real-life events most of us experience. Pro cycling, and all other sports, are entertainments and distractions. They're perfectly valid and valuable and important in those terms. But they're nothing more deep than a game. Quite why we devote so much of our newspapers, websites, radio and television time to sports is beyond me. And I say that as a sports journalist.

However, I am passionate about using your bike as a tool to help you get to grips with the bigger picture. As a way to focus the mind, or relax, or keep you ticking for longer, it is hard to beat. If riding your bike to work gives you more energy to play with the kids, that's great. If going out for a cycle ride helps bring a level of fun to family life, or restore normality to a heated situation, that's excellent. If you find a bike ride helps you think about your job and acts as the catalyst for creative solutions, that's superb, too. In fact, rather than having to find a period of home or family time to fit in a bike ride, I think every employer should allow their staff an hour a day of riding, walking, running, or swimming simply as a way to boost dynamism and efficiency.

How does that fit in with what am I doing here with the old chap? I have to say I'm not sure, although from a personal point of view it's nice to be with dad. On another level, I hope our trip inspires my boys to think about what they can achieve with a little determination. And I'm also hoping that in some small way it'll help with a few of my anxieties and worries. Strangely, it's still that old hypochondria that I feel I need to master most. See, I didn't die of a heart attack up that climb.

So no matter what low moments I've felt at points on this ride, I'm pretty confident there will be some good coming from it. Of course, I could get squashed by an 18-wheeler any minute right now. My kids would be without a dad and my wife left a widow. In which case it was a crap idea to come. But I suppose it's a case of giving yourself acceptable risks. Every day on this ride and in life generally, we have to assume things will work out fine. Otherwise, we'd never get out of bed.

That's certainly the attitude I need to adopt right now with cars and trucks whizzing past. Thankfully we see the signs for La Cavalerie, which is the point where we can get back onto more manageable roads. We branch off and park up outside a boulangerie in the little town.

We stop for breakfast at La Cavalerie, another reminder of our trip in 1994. Back then we came through the town at the end of day nine and camped a little further up the road at l'Hospitalet du Larzac. As usual, nothing looks familiar, other than our breakfast and the tins of Orangina that accompany it. We are obviously in the south of

France, it is jolly hot already. There is hardly anything green growing anywhere. As far as the eye can see all the vegetation has been bleached khaki by the sun.

Nearly every house has its shutters closed to block out the heat, and people only pop out quickly to buy bread. We have a good view of these comings and goings as we park our bums on a window ledge right next to the boulangerie.

I'm despatched to do breakfast duties. There's a fine selection of cakes and an even finer selection of insect life. I opt for some almond croissants and my new favourite, apple chaussons, primarily because they are the only cakes without wasps taking a dump on them.

I bring them out to dad and we eat. If I've learnt anything on this voyage it's that the old chap is extraordinarily fussy about hygiene levels around food. So do I tell him about the creatures kicking about in that cake shop. Er...

"I made sure I picked you the cakes with the least bugs on them," I say, smiling good naturedly. He finishes the cake he's eating, but against type saves the other for later.

We both felt getting out of Millau and surviving the big 'D' road was the last challenge facing us on the road to the Med, but we're proved wrong with a nasty little climb out of La Cavalerie, and from here, the view of a wide open expanse as far as we can see. To our right there is the huge 'N' road motorway, while to our left there's a quiet but fully working airport.

I'm intrigued by the airport, wondering who on earth would ever want to fly into a place like this. From a personal history point of view, that motorway is equally intriguing. Of course it may well have been reclassified since 1994, but last time we were here we actually rode along the hard shoulder of that multi-lane behemoth all the way down and off this plain, even going through the tunnels cut into the hillside. Looking at it now, and mentally looking back, it does lead me to think about whether we should have even been there. I wonder if there are any more fantasy commemorations to the unknown cycle tourists along it. Or failing that, perhaps a 21-year-old local legend about the two ghost cyclists who were seen in the motorway tunnel.

Refueled, we cycle on, always looking for smaller roads with less traffic. We pass our old campsite at l'Hospitalet. It appears it has gone up market: there is not a tent to be seen but in their place are a number of wooden cabins. Maybe it is an activity centre now. We do not stop to find out. The phone box where Matt and I whiled away almost an hour waiting for the person inside to finish their call back in 1994 is still here. I think the fellow must have run out of credit because the box is finally empty.

Day 10 — Death Or Glory

We continue on a small road that runs only yards away from the motorway where trucks and cars fly past at great speed. The area is almost one mass of brown vegetation. Then, on our left, completely in the middle of nowhere, we spot twenty-four crosses and a small memorial.

We do not stop long but I notice that these were members of the resistance who died in August 1944. They were twenty-three members of the Marquis, aged from 18 to 25, who sabotaged the road descending off the Larzac plateau and then decided to take on some of the retreating German columns. They were overwhelmed and ultimately all were killed. The cross on the extreme left in the front row is dedicated to Lieutenant Richard Hoy of the 111th Tactical Reconnaissance Squadron, an American who was shot down and killed while attacking the same German column on the same day.

I don't know if it is the heat, the effort of the journey so far, or the futility of war, but I feel rather emotional. I am no hero and I have only ever seen a couple of dead bodies. It could be said that those corpses looked peaceful, but to me they looked like they were just empty shells that once contained life. By then it's too late for redemption, for either party.

I imagine that your beliefs dictate what happens to you after death. I find it amusing that many people who are getting on in years turn to God. They suddenly go to church, do good deeds and try to lead what could be called a Christian life. It's almost as if they're trying to get some insurance for the future. No one has ever come back to describe the afterlife, if there is one, but these folk want some Brownie points on earth while they still can. Perhaps what I'm saying is mere cynicism. Maybe, like so many other things, you are naturally drawn towards religion as time goes by and it is not intentional after all.

Myself, I have not embraced religion yet. Hopefully I still have plenty of time for that, but personally I rather favour taking a longer-term approach to the size of my welcome at the Pearly Gates. I think all one can hope for is a peaceful death that causes as little distress to others as possible, and which leaves happy memories of a life well-lived.

We cycle towards Le Caylar and — a more pressing unknown than the afterlife right now — possibly some shade. The road goes on and on, and it's very, very hot. In time we start climbing again. It's not noticeably steep, but here and there we get off and walk.

It's all quite slow going. We're drinking huge amounts of water, while birds of prey circle ominously up high. The sky is cloudless and the sun is alive. The Causse de Larzac might be a plateau but there are still hills to contend with. Worst of all, there is simply no shelter.

We spot a grubby young female hitch-hiker at the side of a slip road leading to the motorway. Dad and I are both red-blooded males who haven't seen their wives for 10 days, and this girl isn't unattractive (albeit in need of a good scrub). But the condition we're in right now, neither of us can even muster enough enthusiasm to suggest the cliché that she could ride pillion on the rear rack. Any chat-up line we might consider would be less, 'Can you ride side saddle?' and more likely, 'Any chance you could take a turn on the front?'

An equally grubby middle-aged chap who is desperately trying to hang on to his youth by dying his straggly hair blonde and driving a beaten up purple panel van (I think we all know the type) stops to offer her a lift. I wonder if I need to remember his face for the French version of *Crime Watch*.

Actually, I can forget him. What this young lady lacks in personal grooming she makes up for in common sense and sends him packing. She seems content to wait a little longer. We leave her to it.

Our next stop is Le Caylar and an opportunity to rest up a little. We sit at a picnic table under whatever shade a newly-planted tree can give us and eat an early lunch. We've actually been riding for almost five hours so our body clocks are certainly ready for grub. Dad eats his second cake from this morning while I pop into the Spa store over the road to stock up with more drinks. We're getting through liquid at quite alarming levels today. Meanwhile, every sit down is a chance for our legs to lose enthusiasm. The heat is almost unbearable. We must press on.

From Le Caylar we head down the D9, which begins as a tree-lined boulevard. It's all rather charming while it lasts. Then we're back into the open. Up and around a little hill, and we're into a different world again. As soon as we crested the initial climb out of Millau this morning we realised we were in a landscape quite unlike anything we'd experienced so far, but now everything is turned up to 11. This isn't just barren, this is stark. It's not just arid, it's borderline desert. The trees are leafless, the grass is faded and crisp. Only the gorse bushes retain any vestige of greenery. I hope we'll see a tumbleweed just to complete the vista. There's a low ridge of crags in the hazy distance and at any moment I'm expecting Yul Brynner with half a dozen magnificent pals to come riding over the horizon. I doubt they'd be on touring bikes.

The road is long and straight but it's fine for cycling. Then, out of nowhere the two lanes split, we go right while the oncoming lane goes left. We're descending at good speed. The carriageways reconvene and we head towards the very small outpost of humanity at Saint Pierre de la Fage. As if it couldn't get any more like a scene from a Western, Saint Pierre even has an old, squat windmill welcoming us. This truly is like death valley.

We follow a relatively green slice of land onwards, there's even a bit of shade, but we're both still suffering. We park up underneath a tree at the foot of the climb out of the village and perch on the dry stone wall for a little respite. Not for the first time on this journey I take the Buff off of my head and ring the sweat out. Dad's gone well all trip but I think he's pretty much reached his limit. I check the weather — it's currently 34 degrees. For the first time he talks about where we'll camp up tonight. From the map, it shouldn't be too far. We've got a bit more of the Causse de Larzac to do then a descent to either Saint André or Gignac.

It's a desperate effort. The land we encounter once beyond the village isn't quite as austere as before — there seems to be a few more trees and bushes, and the grass appears just a little more lush, although that's not hard to achieve — but it's not without its own points of interest. The one that grabs me most is a huge installation off to our left, eastwards, perched atop the biggest cliff in the area. It has a massive antenna (or is that a rocket-launching platform?) and wouldn't be out of place as a Bond baddy's lair. We know the French are keen on military kit and nuclear technology, so I dread to think what it is — I hope it's just a TV or radio transmitting station.

The trees grow thicker, the road weaves between low rocks, we see a sign marking the 'Col du Vent 703m' and suddenly everything opens up in front of us. It feels as if all of southern France lies ahead. We can see the rim of the Causse disappearing to our right, while countless other lesser hills strive to make a mark just ahead. Dusty roads thread their way around them. We might not reach Sète today but this is the moment when I know we'll make it. We will survive.

I spot a lizard perched on a rock nearby. I wonder if I can get close to take a shot of it with my phone. I'd expect it to scamper off as soon as it sees me approach but, c'est la France, even the reptiles can't be arsed and it sits there while I get within centimetres. I take a swig of water from my bottle but it's so warm it feels like drinking butter. Up here, in almost complete silence, the sound of crickets dominates.

Time for fun, a big descent. The road winds downwards, hairpinning right then left. Sadly our progress is only lateral: the slope directs us from side to side, east to west, it doesn't take us any further south towards Sète. I enjoy it, though, and stop to take some photos. We drop more than 2,000 feet in nine miles but dad's not having a good time.

What goes up has to come down, and the prospect of several kilometres of comfortable descending brightens up our next five minutes. I'm afraid the idea of dreamy downhills with miles of fast freewheeling remain only in the imagination, though. It's true, we have a great descent that should be easy, but the roads are far from smooth. In fact, they are a catalogue of half-hearted repairs and the combination of very bumpy surfaces and constant application of the brakes make my forearms ache. I have to stop every now and then to find some respite.

Matt takes some photos on the way down and at the bottom of this, the longest descent of the trip, we are reunited. With its hairpin bends separated by long straight stretches, this could have been a stereotypical mountainside descent. We just needed a few dark tunnels to complete the effect, and preferably something expensive with four wheels and an engine.

The heat increases and the road levels out again. We are both exhausted and, with Sète a further 30 miles away, we decide the best option is to abandon today's efforts at Gignac.

Everything feels a little different after coming down off the mountain. It's not like the barren moonscape above, and it's not like the lush green France we enjoyed before descending to Millau yesterday. The buildings, when we see any, are all Mediterranean looking. Grapes are growing, and there are some low hills in the distance. For now, they are tomorrow's problem.

Eventually we see road signs for Gignac. Our first port of call has to be somewhere to buy food, and here — after possibly the most removed-from-civilisation day we've had — we find the biggest and best supermarket sitting proudly among car dealerships and home improvement megastores. I go in and stock up with supplies, knowing we have the luxury of only being a few hundred yards from the campsite. It's not all hunky dory: for the first time on this trip I start to worry I'll show too much in my Lycra cycle shorts. Proof that once the real concerns have past, my mind will create some new ones to taunt me. Thankfully the rest of my body doesn't have the energy to pump blood anywhere other than where it's truly needed.

We load the grub on the bikes and head to the campsite. It's easy to find and dad speaks to a bloke who seems to be in charge. He's straight out of a *Carry On...* movie, too. A dirty, grubby little beggar who won't look dad in the eye and demands he takes the old chap's passport off with him until 5pm when we can pay. Sweet lord, after 10 days with 'Papa Paranoia' I know where this is going to go.

However, before the little berk clears off he offhandedly tilts his head to a patch of what looks like cat litter. Apparently that is where we can camp. At least it's under some shade. Oh, and like last night, it's the last pitch available. Aren't we lucky?

The campsite is an interesting facility. We get the last pitch apparently, and it is shady as requested. But instead of grass there is gravel underfoot. I think this is another place geared up for camping cars rather than tents. However, we are not going anywhere else, so it has to do.

Unusually, the campsite proprietor takes my passport away with him and tells me to meet him at his 'office' at 17.00hrs, when I can pay him. It has been a long day, so we set up camp. Most of our previous campsites have had soil that was difficult to plunge tent pegs into, but this one is exceptional. We are forced to search around for rocks to replace tent pegs. It's not a particularly successful approach: every time we bump into a guy rope it becomes dislodged.

Despite having had his passport swiped, dad is impressively calm. We wait until 5pm and then the old chap goes to pay and retrieve his ID. He comes back unimpressed: it's the most expensive pitch yet. But hey ho.

He tells me something about the dirty fellow and it's obvious they have had a chat. I say surely after seeing the state of this country, dad's not still going on about his French heritage.

"I always tell them that, and that we're from Jersey. They bloody hate the English," he replies.

"I wonder why they're so keen on Liptons ice tea, then?" I postulate.

The old chap doesn't miss a breath. "Well, that's because they go gaga for English stuff." Sometimes he doesn't even see his own illogicality.

As I say, it is an unusual site. Everywhere possible there is a sign, either advertising postcards, chips or hamburgers, or posting a warning of some likely mishap. It has a swimming pool, too, so by the standards of the day it is very luxurious. This is further brought home to me when I pay. This site, with its gravel pitch, costs us just under 25 euros for one night! Easily the most expensive site of the trip. But after our stay at Chasseneuil du Poitou, I have come to the conclusion that the cost must to be inversely proportional to the quality of the site. Still, it is a small price to be reunited with my passport.

Finally, certain we're going to spend the night here, I go for a shower. Dad can't be bothered to wash, so he waits for me to get back then we eat — a proper good nosh-up this evening. We speak to mum and Manda. By 7pm dad's already going to sleep and I can hear myself getting stroppy because he wants both the tent's inner and outer doors closed for security and to keep away mozzies. But there are mozzies already in the tent with us and it's still 28 degrees outside even now. It's so hot, I'm sweating just lying down.

Once he's dropped off to nodsville I open the inner tent door for a token amount of air but I still can't sleep. I'm planning tomorrow's route and there are children enjoying themselves outside, running to and from the pool. I hear the old fella stir a bit, I look over and see him squinting at his watch. He turns in panic, "Matt! Matt! it's 8 o'clock. We've got to get up!" he exclaims.

"Yes dad, it's 8 o'clock from the night before. Don't worry." He turns back and drops off. With the stony ground poking through our groundsheet and sleeping mats, the kids running around outside, and this almost unbearable heat, I have to admire his ability.

We eat and I am shattered, so I retire to bed at the exceptionally early hour of 18.30hrs. It is so hot that all I can do is lie on my Thermarest mattress, in my cycling shorts, and perspire. I think that I must have nodded off because at 20.00hrs I look at my watch and tell Matt it is time to get up. He had not even gone to bed, it is still evening.

It's at moments like this that your mind races through abstract thoughts that you'd never bother with during the day. The idea that the French were keen cyclists and loved anyone on a bike is one that I am having particular difficulty with. This fallacy bugged me during the day and more especially now when I have nothing else to concern myself with.

By now we've cycled more than 550 miles across France, but have I seen swarms of old ladies or even old gentlemen gliding along on fat-tyred utility bikes? No. What I have seen is the odd aged roadie or 'coureur' in club strip, pedalling along on a venerable steel racing bike. And we did see a group of club riders on day five using bikes that were more modern.

I am left with the impression that France's regular cyclists are more Raymond Poulidor than Romain Bardet. And given the choice, nowadays most French would prefer to ride in a Renault rather than pedal a Peugeot.

Eventually I go back to sleep.

So we didn't get to Sète in 10 days, but we had a good stab. Tomorrow should be little more than a leisurely spin to the seaside.

Day 10 — Death Or Glory

RIDES OF PASSAGE

DAY 11
Return Of The Med(i)

Wednesday August 12, 2015 — Gignac to Sète (29.3 miles)

Matt aged 36

OK, so we haven't got down to the Mediterranean in 10 days like last time but I'm not disappointed. I don't know how we managed it in 1994. Between the heat, the busier roads, and not being quite as full of youthful vigour, I reckon 10 days and hopefully just a few more hours is still pretty good going.

As always, it's an early start, but the sun is thwarting us in a different way this morning. Despite both dad and me waking at 6am there's no light outside until 6.45, so we can't get away until 7.40. That should be plenty good enough. It is due to be hot again today but we aim to be in Sète well before lunch.

Arthur aged 63

Here, down south, the nights are as cold as the days are hot, so it's no surprise that I woke up very, very early this morning shivering. Naturally, being a responsible parent I did not want to wake Matt up, so I avoided searching for my sleeping bag inside my pannier, which was outside the tent anyway. It was freezing so I put on my fleece gilet, which I have used throughout the trip as a pillow. I was slightly warmer.

Once properly awake, we take down the tent and pack up quickly because there are no pegs to struggle with today. Soon we are ready to go. When there is sufficient light the chorus of cicadas strikes up at exactly 08.00hrs. It's as if they work in shifts; one lot sings from daybreak until 3pm, then another crew comes on duty and keeps up the racket until nightfall.

In my haste I forget my hi-tech washing line: four metres of nylon cord that cost me about 90 pence and which I've cherished throughout the trip. It has been indispensable: we have both done our washing every day and we've always needed somewhere reliable to hang it. Looking on the positive side, I suppose I won't require it any more.

Soon on the road and today's mileage promises to be minimal. We had hoped to reach Sète yesterday, but 80 miles in that heat would have been impossible. So far it is still quite cool and we can make good progress. We stop at a crossroads for a photo call. There is a lone shed in one corner of a nearby field, so I dive behind it to pee. With three roads converging on this spot, it is only a three to one chance that anyone will pass me. No guesses from which direction the only car we've seen in five minutes comes from. I've got nothing to be ashamed of. As we discovered back on day six I am able to switch lights on with this! And we're in France, of course, so peeing in public is quite normal behaviour.

There's a fair blanket of cloud above and to begin with the roads are in our favour. We head past my favourite supermarket from last night and then we're on long, flat, tree-lined avenues with fields of grapes lying beyond. The land is certainly well-worked in France, although I have no clue by whom. We've passed hundreds of fields, yet we've only actually seen a dozen or so farm workers. I remove the hub dynamo whose grating noise has been plaguing me since Saint Malo. It has done its job, but not without a lot of complaint.

By 8.30am the sun is breaking through and we've reached the lower slopes of our first hill of the day: a 400-foot blip on the run down to the sea. We stop at the side of a road for a pre-climb drink. There are plenty of cars going past, although we realise one has stopped behind us. It's a massive white Citroen estate driven by what I can only describe as two bleach-blonde French Essex girls, neither of whom are in the first flush of youth. They sound their horn and gesticulate to us to move even further out of the way — if we do that, we'll be down the side of the embankment.

I have had enough. Enough of these people particularly. And enough of France in general. I step into the road, raise the middle finger of my right hand, and shout some choice Anglo-Saxon phrases directly at them.

I blame this heated outburst on my fabled Gallic heritage.

Instantly, I'm ashamed. I have let myself down. I flipped them the bird. Yet we are in France, and I am an honorary Englishman. If ever there was a moment to summon the spirit of Agincourt and display two digits, rampant, it was now. I'm afraid rage got the better of my senses.

Just to put my mind at ease, dad suggests they might not even have been French. I consider this for a second, but then justify it thus: who else but a French person would be driving a brand-new 30ft Citroen barge?

So, with adrenaline coursing through my veins, buoyed by the fact that we are now on the home run, and having possibly offended parents, cyclists, Jersey residents, cycle journalists, drivers of German cars, the French and anybody else I can think of so far on this journey, let's have a crack at truly the most fearsome sector of all: women cyclists.

Over the years I've thought a lot about women's cycling, mainly because some of the fiercest, most antagonistic letters we receive as cycling journalists come from ladies. Often it's a case of asking us why there aren't more women depicted in cycling mags, or why more articles aren't written directly for women. Maybe I'm too simple but they leave me very confused because cycling is a universal pleasure, and whether it's an article about diet, or technique, or fitness, the ideas being explained should be just as applicable to female riders as they are to male cyclists.

I also have to say that, in my experience of the magazines I've worked for, women have been represented pretty well both in editorial staff and in photographic content. Certainly, compared to how many female cyclists actually read cycling mags, it's extremely positive. Market research tends to show that around 85 per cent of mainstream cycling magazines are read by men — and I'm being ultra conservative here, I know that in many specific cases male readership is way above 90 per cent. But even though appealing to women readers is about as sensible as an advertising agency being asked to hit the male market for Vagisil, the cycling media does try its best to be as universal as possible.

One incident pretty much sums up how I feel. Over the last couple of years I've been the editor of a magazine called *What Cycle?* It is purely a bike review mag — a fairly innocuous subject one would think. But last year I had a letter from an irate female reader who said she had bought a copy and felt it was an awful waste of money because we hadn't tested any women's bikes.

I emailed back to ask her what a woman's bike was? In my opinion, bicycles and human beings conform to fairly universal dimensions albeit in a range of sizes. I know a women's bike isn't one simply painted in pink, purple or white because so many experienced female cyclists have told me these colours are patronising (although these experienced riders should perhaps have a word with novice female cyclists whose priorities tend to be a little different and seem to put colour at the top of their requirements). So how could a typical women's bike differ from a typical male rider's bike?

Well it might have to be smaller because women tend to be smaller. But then so would a bike required by a small man. It might have to be lighter because women aren't as strong as men. But then no bike manufacturer purposely makes any bike heavier than it has to be. We've already ascertained that colour shouldn't come into it. What about the frame then — are men and women's body shapes different?

The biggest difference in male and female physiology, so we're often told, is found in relative leg length to overall height. Women's legs are supposed to be proportionally longer by a fraction. But not so much that it would require a recalculation of a bike frame's basic dimensions.

However, I've chatted about this with a lot of top bike designers and that old leg-length-thing is really used as a way to sugarcoat a slightly different pill. If you go into the detail of the difference between men's and women's bodies, the truth is that women actually have their weight lower down. There's no way to say this nicely — they have heavier bottoms. Men have bigger, heavier chests and shoulders.

So, to make a woman's bike more suitable having taken this into account, you might want to change the frame shape a fraction compared to a man's bike. But can you ever see a bicycle manufacturer saying, "Actually, we've built our women's bikes differently to take into account women's heavier bottoms"? Nope.

In any case, a bit of tweaking with components such as stem length and saddle position should overcome all of this, and any correctly-sized non-women-specific bike should be perfectly comfortable and useable for any rider. First and foremost, it's the sizing that's important.

There is one area where change in equipment is required between the sexes: saddle choice. Women cyclists can suffer from groin numbness to an even greater extent than male riders, and cycle manufacturers have come up with a range of effective saddle options for female riders.

I would also argue that women have proportionally wider hips so might benefit from a wider Q-Factor or stance width — the distance laterally between foot placement on the pedals. However, I'm a little ahead of the game there — I don't see any manufacturers focusing on this area, and I don't hear women cyclists even talking about it. Smaller brake and gear levers would also help, too, but again I don't see Shimano or SRAM rushing any women-specific products out, although you can now fit little shims inside the brake lever to bring the levers closer.

So my message for women cyclists is simple, and it's the same as I'd give to a male cyclist: buy a bike that fits and find a good saddle. Almost every other concern is shared by all of us who cycle.

I hope that's not controversial and I'm not going to get hit by another round of awful letters. But then again — as I know — so few women read cycling publications I'm probably safe to say what I like here! What's this got to do with cycle touring? Nothing really, it was just something I was thinking about it.

We keep climbing up this quite tough little hill, although the aggressive excitement of earlier and the sense that we're nearing our ultimate goal have us spinning at a decent pace. We don't enjoy much of a view at the summit, although we're soon heading back down on a wide, curving road and I stop to take a shot of an awesome wind farm to our left. We remount, but only for 100 metres. As we come round the hill the landscape opens up ahead of us and we can finally see all the way to Sète. It's our first glimpse of the ocean since Saint Malo. I stop and take another photo.

There is a repeat of a problem that I suffered from on the last day of our original trip, which is that you expect to see the sea around the next corner. There are still hills but, as the route gets flatter, you imagine it will be easy to see that far into the distance. In practice it does not work that way. Although we do see the sea much sooner than last time, it is still miles away.

It's at times like these, and there have been plenty of moments like this during our tour, that you have to have patience. At least we are descending towards the sea, the road is well surfaced, and we even have a cycle lane. Just keep pedalling and wait a little longer.

Is this kind of attitude the key to success in life? I suppose it depends on what you define success to be. There are many areas in which we can succeed, and most of them are purely personal.

As I've got older, the world seems to have got just a little more self-centred, and personal triumphs and happiness are nothing unless backed up by an immense and very visible collection of material possessions (ideally supported by an overriding aura of pretension). I believe that this is the modern, commonly accepted face of 'success'. What is it that the very ostentatious say? "What I have is only a score card for what I've achieved." Urgh. Perhaps surprisingly, a great deal of 'high achievers' do not do what they do solely for the money. They are driven to want to be the fastest, the biggest, the most profitable, the best known, or sometimes even the most popular. That last one can be a drain on all the other benchmarks, though, irrespective of any tangible gain.

Another thing that is often forgotten along the way is the amount of personal and family sacrifice that has to be made to reach these successes. There is often a totally focused and single-minded approach that high achievers take in attaining their goals, regardless of the fallout along the way. This is important. How often have you seen someone who is not overly clever, excel at something? They may have some God-given talents, but these are not always enough to put them in the top echelons of whatever they do. What they lack in brains is made up for by sheer determination. Ignorance can be a benefit, too — it's possible that many others have been in the same situation, but have seen the potential pitfalls and have tried something else.

When it comes to the path we tread, help and advice can be dangerous. Particularly unhelpful is when the person doing the advising would have liked to have been successful at something themselves. In the bike shop, I'd see parents or grandparents spending thousands of pounds on equipment for their progeny to dabble in, without the kids having any real interest at all. It is a difficult, costly and totally unnecessary situation that many families find themselves in. The children tend to go along with it to make their folks happy, or because it may be quite a glamorous pastime for a while. But in the end it is the road to nowhere. In fact, this approach is often a surefire way to put the child off that activity for life.

Of course, what you like doing, and what you are good at, can be two entirely different things. Here we arrive at another stumbling block for the *common idea of success: what if you are totally hopeless at say, motorcycle trials (I'm thinking of myself here), but you enjoy it immensely? It makes you happy, even though going by official results you are terrible and easily the worst rider there. Where does happiness come in the success stakes?*

Let's bring it back to what Matt and I are doing here on these last stretches of road before we reach our goal in Sète. This cycle tour isn't an earth-shattering achievement; it really could be done by a huge number of people if they were to put their minds to it. But for all the trials and tribulations on this trip, I have to view it as an obvious success. We aimed to ride across France again, and we've done it. I've enjoyed it, despite the physical pressures along the way. We haven't really had to trample on anyone's feelings or happiness to do it. And, perhaps most importantly, we can justifiably enjoy that strange contentedness and pride that comes with completing a goal you set yourself but weren't entirely sure you could achieve.

Ultimately, I'd have to say that being happy is the only real measure of success. Right now, with the end in sight, I feel happy that we did this, but also happy that we're almost finished.

We descend and head past the town of Villeveyrac. It's a pretty busy and unpleasant 'D' road afterwards, and again there's a soul-sapping little climb, but soon we've taken a right turn and we're heading south. The road is a delight and there are moments when we could be in a Cézanne painting. The road into Poussan particularly reminds me of one of his Jas de Buffon pictures. We pass through the town centre and there's more art — a picture of Elvis graffitied on a wall — before we have to negotiate a series of big roads and roundabouts.

Incredibly, we're soon pedalling next to water. And for once it's sea water, not a river. Last night, while plotting our route, I was worried about this stretch. It's the main artery into Sète and I remember it being heavy with traffic 21 years ago. This time, though, there's a handy cycle lane running alongside.

The water is a deep blue, the sun is bright and the sky is clear. We're approaching the Mediterranean, it should be a picture postcard moment. Yet everything we're passing is evidence of heavy industry, or faceless retail warehouses such as car dealerships and megastores. It is, in a nutshell, an industrial hell-hole.

Eventually the cycle lane peters out and we have to join the traffic over the bridge into Sète. We're in no rush and sit patiently — two large chaps on scooters aren't so keen to wait and take to buzzing on the pavement to get further on. Riding a motorcycle on the pavement? C'est la France.

We pass through a built-up area called Balaruc le Vieux which hides Sète and its lagoon, and it comes as a surprise when we suddenly find ourselves beside the sea, the boats and our finishing point in the near distance.

Gradually we get nearer and nearer. We wait in the long queue of cars as the swing bridge admits only a few at a time into the town. There is no urgency for us any longer, we've arrived. The easy ride in helps us to remember the place; the train station, the boats, and across the bridge ahead, our hotel. It is 10.30hrs and the whole place looks even better than last time.

We make it over the bridge and we can see Sète's canals and pretty streets ahead. I try to work out where we chatted to the old Statler and Waldorf characters on the bench 21 years ago. Then we pass the train station; we must bank that in our memories for tomorrow. We have a hotel booked — the Grand Hotel, where we stayed on our last day in 1994 — so we head towards it. It's just about the prettiest building in the town, so it's easy to spot.

We go inside and the friendly lady behind the reception desk says our room isn't ready yet — it's still just before 11am — but we can park the bikes up in the foyer if we want. We do that, locking them together, and take our handlebar bags with all their precious things inside with us.

Sète seems to be a mix of 1970s' architecture, Art Noveau, and French Colonial, all basking under a southern sun. It is a painter's paradise, the light off the water is magical and the colours seem more vivid. Our hotel is definitely Art Noveau, the columns that hold up the porch swirl skywards and you would not be surprised if Poirot suddenly appeared in a doorway.

Despite the age of most of the inhabitants, Sète seems quite a trendy place, and although quite old, no one actually appears infirm. There does seem to be a high concentration of chemists, orthopaedic suppliers and chiropractors in town, so maybe this is what keeps the population mobile.

We receive a warm welcome at the Grand Hotel. Unlike last time they are expecting us. However, just like last time we resemble two unshaven cycling vagabonds. They allow us to leave our bikes in the entrance, behind the front doors, while we go to get something to eat.

Sète is heaving with people and we try to hang on to the pavement. Dad's not quite into his full aimlessly-walking-at-speed stride, but he's getting there. I stop him on a bridge over one of the canals and we take a selfie just to prove we really made it. With that important job done it's time to find something to eat. There's no shortage of restaurants but we just need a sandwich, so we go looking for a supermarket or something similar.

We find one along a main street. It's a small chainstore mini-mart, but it'll do. We go inside and pick out some drinks and ready-made sandwiches. I go to pay. Throughout our little journey dad has very kindly been giving me little crappy bits of eurocents shrapnel that he didn't want to trouble himself with, and I've been keeping them in a small zipped bag that used to contain my now long-lost travel towel. With no other customers in the shop, it seems a perfect chance to get rid of all this change.

I hand over our purchases to a large middle-aged man with greasy shoulder length hair and a bright, floral, Hawaiian-style shirt. I'm not one to judge — ahem — but even by French standards he is quite obviously a loser. I start counting out the change. There is no queue behind. Yet 'Monsieur Fun-guy' starts tapping the counter impatiently, muttering "Vite, vite!" I raise my head and look him in the eye without even trying to conceal my anger.

"It has taken us 11 days to get here," I say quite calmly. "You can bloody well wait."

I think he understands enough English to get the message, putting his arms up at his side in mock surrender and saying, "Pardon." C'est la France.

We take our sandwiches to a bench next to the water and watch two elderly gentlemen fishing. They're in luck and we see them retrieve a couple of decent size mackerel. Were it not for the lingering aroma of dog dirt from the pavement, this would almost be idyllic.

By the time we get back to the hotel, our room is ready.

When we return, Matt checks in and takes our key. We take a lift up to the third floor and, with four pannier bags each, squeeze along the atrium balconies that run above the restaurant and service the rooms around the edge. Matt fights with the lock to get it open but the room itself is nice and in the shade. The windows are open, but the shutters are drawn to prevent the sun blazing in. It is cool inside, there is a television, an en-suite bathroom, and the whole place exudes style.

We've made it, what a joyous feeling.

Once in the room, I lie on the bed and remain immobile for an eternity. Finally, I rouse myself and go to the loo to inspect the damage. I discover something a little surprising: my cotton wool padding isn't there. It must have slipped out on the ride here this morning. For me personally, that seems a fitting legacy: somewhere in the corner of a French field, there is a rancid cotton wool pad that has been cradling a Jerseyman's injured and sweaty balls but which is forever England.

But this journey hasn't been about me against France; it's been about dad and me, together. In the days, weeks, month and years to come we'll be able to look back on this adventure with a far more rosy hue than is possible right now. However, we got through it. There may have been times of strain, but for two men who only actually see each other twice a year, to manage the heat, the distance, the tiredness and the exertion of the last 11 days not just loving but actually still liking each other is a fair achievement.

I can honestly say I would not and could not have done this ride with anyone else. And to my mind, there cannot be a better testament to a father and son's relationship than that.

So, will I do it again with my own boys? Right now, I'd say no chance. But give me 21 years to think about it.

Day 11 — Return Of The Med(i)

Afterword

Matt aged 36

So what came after Sète? A difficult journey to Saint Malo by train, where we had to contend with the officiousness of SNCF staff. An early morning ferry ride back to Jersey. And finally, cuddles with Manda, mum and the boys at the harbour — exactly where we'd parted almost two weeks before.

Over the following days the pain of my unmentionables happily receded until they became unnoticeables. I rapidly regained whatever weight I had lost while cycling 600 miles in 35-degree heat. And I vowed never to ride a bike again. So very much business as usual.

But did I learn anything deeper from the experience?

There's a line in this book where dad is talking about the pilgrims we saw at Livinhac Le Haut and he says something about them looking for enlightenment while we are just hoping for a warm shower and something to eat. He was quite right. When we planned and set out on this 2015 cycle tour, I don't think either of us were expecting to discover much about ourselves that we didn't already know. We just thought it would be interesting — I hesitate to use the word 'fun' — to repeat the challenge of cycling across France.

Going into the ride, I had my eyes open. I knew I wasn't particularly keen on really suffering on a bike, so the reality came no surprise. I knew I'd miss my wife and children and home, so that was no great discovery, either. And I was more than aware the old chap would be, at times, a little strange. The depth of the challenge we faced was greater than expected, but essentially I understood that at some point I'd get fromaged-off.

Certainly one thing I've realised since writing and then reading (and re-reading and re-reading) *Rides of Passage* is what a bloody misery I appear. This I find very odd. In real-life I'm generally quite a cheery chap, although what's going on in my sub-conscious is anyone's guess. But in my defence, I can only suggest that during this particular 11-day period all the things I like least colluded with a few unforeseen difficulties to give me a bit of a kicking.

Of course, the experience was far from being all bad. The chance to look back at some of our 2015 trans-France photographs has already caused dad and me to start reminiscing almost fondly. Unfortunately we can't wax too lyrical as both Manda and mum are quick to remind us of the despair we (and by 'we', I mean mainly 'I') felt, in the process nipping any glorious memories in the bud. It's fair to say our rose-tinted spectacles are quickly knocked from our faces, their lenses promptly shattered, and any remaining glass is ground into a fine dust by two dainty pairs of size five shoes.

However, there is something that this incredible journey has made me think about. So let me tell you a story.

A few years ago, shortly after the boys were born, I went to try out at a local shooting club because I wanted to see if I still had any talent with a rifle. I met a motley collection of folk, and I particularly remember one rather bawdy old man who was always going on in a lecherous way about young women. I must have given him a disapproving look, because I can recall him good-naturedly explaining: "The thing is, just because I'm old, it doesn't mean I've stopped feeling like a young bloke who fancies pretty girls. It's just that I can't do as much about it nowadays."

Our cycle tour has brought home exactly what that chap meant. Riding across France with dad really did put me back in the mindset of being the teenager I was in 1994 and I was able to remember the hopes and dreams I once had of meeting young ladies, learning to drive, and going to university. Back then I certainly wasn't thinking about getting married, having a job, and being a dad, although now all that — and more — has come to pass. I'd love to do it again, it was great fun, however time has moved on and in many respects that's a bittersweet feeling.

But while life happens and the world around us is transformed, reliving this experience has made me think that, like that old geezer in the shooting club, mentally perhaps we never really change. Reading our modern ride accounts side-by-side with our journals from 1994, it's hilarious to see just how similarly we reacted to the things that occurred. The reality is that, despite being 21 years older, there were plenty of times during this 11-day journey across France when I might as well have been that 15-year-old son again. I'm sure there were moments when the old chap felt like a 42-year-old dad again, or even a teenage cyclist himself, too.

At the start of this book we quote from *The Picture of Dorian Gray*: "To get back one's youth, one has merely to repeat one's follies." It's not far from the truth, at least to the person committing the follies. The thing I learned on this trip is that we each have our own versions of the picture of Dorian Grey, an image of ourselves that never ages, painted on the canvas of our psyche. Of course, the rest of the world only sees the physical image of us, which is subject to the effects of ageing. To many people who yearn after eternal youth, that is a sad situation: we can't stop the onset of time, no matter how much we try or delude ourselves.

However, two things, give me hope.

The first is seeing the old chap, who for all his self-deprecating behaviour — after all, he christened himself 'the old chap', not us — clings onto his inner Dorian Gray better than most and carries on doing what he enjoys, with very little regard to age. He might be a little more creaky getting up in the morning, but I'm not sure he's ever really changed much since he was a boy.

The second great hope is to remember that time, like distance, is a journey. The more interesting we can make it and the more challenging the experiences, the better the memories and the greater the satisfaction.

But I would still recommend keeping a pair of rose-coloured spectacles nearby just in case.

Arthur aged 63

Well, it has been almost seven months since our French trip and, as they say, 'time is a great healer'. So by now all the injuries and aches and pains have disappeared, and only the mental scars remain. I no longer wake up in the middle of the night reliving the escalator incident. This happened on the way back, so it never appeared in the book. It's probably sufficient to say there was a sign indicating: 'No prams or pushchairs on the escalator', but there was no mention of fully loaded touring bikes.

In many ways, we are now in the same state as when the madcap plan was hatched. It does not take very long to forget the heat, the cars, the hills and camping every night; so you can imagine how easy we thought it was going to be with a gap of 21 years clouding our judgement.

All that aside, I have to address the immediate past and say how it was and what, if anything, I have learned from the trip. I think that there were plenty of lessons to take and it was really surprising that we did not pick them up the first time around, although in fairness, I do believe that France has changed massively in the intervening years. Certainly the original 1994 route is now obsolete, and we diverted from it at any opportunity. I believe that this is due to an increase in the vehicle population more than anything else; certainly the roads are now so busy that the 'D' roads suggested in our route guide are no fun at all.

The campsites are much better. Nearly all the toilets were modern and actually had flushing facilities. In 1994, I remember many loos were of the 'put your feet here, and rely on gravity' type. In addition to this, all the campsites had showers and I never saw any women hosing the urinals down, as witnessed in our previous trip. I did not see any rats either, which must be a pointer to an improvement of standards. In fact, the camping was not too bad, if you forgive the odd rock solid pitch that no tent pegs could ever penetrate.

This time our sleeping arrangements were also better. Matt had his own sleeping mat, which was rather narrow, but despite this he soldiered on and I never had to give him mine. Our sleeping bags were perfectly suitable, although in the final nights it was incredibly hot to begin with, then around 2am it got very, very cold and a sleeping bag was welcome.

The food was good, too. I think that Matthew feared starvation, so he took it upon himself to stock up at any chance. All this cycling places a big demand on calories, so it's almost impossible to put on any weight. In fact, even though you're eating at any opportunity, I at least, seemed to lose weight. This goes back on quickly when you return to civilisation and home comforts.

So what have I, or indeed anyone else, learnt from this last odyssey across France? Before I forget completely, it was quite hard, but some of that was produced by the schedule that we set ourselves. I always said that I'd like to do it again but at a slower pace. We did do it more slowly, but only by half a day or so. I was rather thinking of two weeks or more, so that you could soak in the atmosphere, enjoy the moment and appreciate all that 'La Belle France' can offer.

As I found previously, a generous amount of preparation time is never wasted and often can prevent a few foreseeable problems. I'm happy to report that we had no mechanical breakdowns at all — not even a puncture — during our 1,000 kilometre ride. This was quickly remedied when I returned home: I had two punctures within the first week back!

The other thing that resounded with both of us, particularly Matt, was that you never, never ever, use a brand new Brooks saddle on a trip of this length. The injuries that Matt had to suffer were really unnecessary and they turned a usually easy-going companion into a rather unhappy chap.

Notwithstanding his saddle/bottom interface problems, he made a magnificent job of guiding us through France, finding food and coping with the often unusual approach to things that his father has. He also sourced much of our equipment, booked the trains, and paid for the hotels.

In fact, it was quite a case of role reversal from our original trip, as Matt made all the pre-travel arrangements and he plotted our route as we went. So frankly, I found it much easier than last time, and as Matthew is now in his thirties, he should probably take charge any way.

I can only imagine that this switch in authority must reflect the fact that the intervening years have naturally produced a number of changes in Matthew's approach to things. This is quite normal, and indeed to be expected as he journeys through life. Marriage, fatherhood and all the other challenges that life presents shape the man we see today, and if I was still 'in charge' I would be worried.

Acknowledgements

Matt would like to thank

I think we should point out that we offered to buy all the kit we chose to use on this ride and we did indeed pay for most of it. However, many of our friends in the welcoming world of the UK bike industry still helped a lot. So thank you to Gareth Evans, James Olsen, Chris Snook and Magdalena Schoerner at Evans Cycles; John Harrison and Doreen at Lusso; Loz Cox at Dawes; everyone at Madison; John Pocklington and Colin Thomson at Spa Cycles; Nils Amelinckx at Lyon/Ortlieb; Ewan MacGregor at CycleWiz; Chris Stuckey at Extra UK/Brooks; Sam Jones and Victoria Hazael at CTC/Cycling UK; and the legend who is Mike Burrows. Also, a huge thanks to my UK 'mechanic' Kaye Patton. Kaye is every cyclist's dream woman — as good at building bikes as she is at baking cakes.

There are a few people over the last 21 years who have all played an important part in keeping me more or less sane. So in a vaguely chronological order, my very personal thanks to Stu Nicolle, Will Millow, Chris Godden, Chris Turner, Howard Banks, Dimitris Tsarouhas, Ian Barker, Dan Thomas, James Shrubsall, Simon Smythe, Simon Hursthouse, Luke Edwardes-Evans, Robert Garbutt, Ben Smith, Patrick Trainor, Andy Jones, Catchy Pole, DG, Jason Hardy, Sarah Auld, Andy Lulham and Tracey Mangan.

Special mention must also go to my good friends Callum Tomsett, the greatest designer in the cycling press, who created the front cover and laid out the pages for this book; and Nigel Wynn, who proof read the final version and — as far I'm aware — has never let anyone down in his entire life.

Finally, as always my biggest thanks go to my family for their unstinting support and patience: Ritchie, Clare, Felix, Ernie, Jane, Mum, Adam, David and Manda.

Oh yes, and Mr Arthur P. Lamy. So then, what's next?

Arthur's grateful acknowledgements

This is rather like accepting an Oscar, all very embarrassing for everyone concerned, and I'll no doubt forget to mention someone extremely important, and I'll try not to cry.

For putting up with all my madcap schemes, especially this one, and proof-reading, sub-editing and censoring this book, my dear wife Susan Lamy (Mrs).

For providing us with our dream Ortlieb panniers and handlebar bags, which were completely waterproof, easy to use, and wipe clean, Lyon Outdoor (www.lyon.co.uk/outdoor).

Acknowledgements

For supplying us with seriously well-padded bib shorts, which allowed me to use Matthew's brand new Brooks leather saddle for most of the trip without any injuries at all, Lusso (www.lusso.bike).

For providing me (when I worked in a bike shop) with most of the other stuff that I used on this trip — albeit at trade prices — a plethora of cycle representatives.

For letting us use his fantastic photo of two idiots up a rock, Danny Evans.

Lastly, I must thank my eldest son Matthew, for not only asking me along, but also booking the trains, planning the route, purchasing items of equipment and making sure that we ate regularly.

Apparently I drove him mad, so apologies for that, but as my wife would agree: 'at least I'm never boring'.